Merry Christmas—

YOU'RE FIRED!

By George Allen

With Charles Maher

SIMON AND SCHUSTER / NEW YORK

Library of Congress Cataloging in Publication Data

Allen, George Herbert, date.
   Merry Christmas—you're fired!

   Includes bibliographical references.
   1. Allen, George Herbert, date.   2. Football
coaches—United States—Biography.   3. Job hunting—
United States.   I. Maher, Charles.   II. Title.
GV939.A53A35   1982   796.332'092'4 [B]   82-5862
ISBN 0-671-43837-9   AACR2

Permission of the following to reprint from published works is gratefully
acknowledged.

   Woman's Day: "How to Weather Unemployment," by Maxine
Schnall, October 14, 1980.
   Newsweek: "How It Feels to Be Out of Work," by Jan Halvorsen, in
the column "My Turn," September 22, 1980.
   The Washington Post: "Frank Kush in Exile: Days of Future Past,"
by John Feinstein, October 4, 1981.
   Los Angeles Times: "Out of a Job: Transition's Bitter Pill," by Bryce
Nelson, April 12, 1981.

(Continued on page 235)

2173144

ACKNOWLEDGMENTS

The author wishes to extend his thanks to William Warren, who was most helpful in the early stages of the writing of this book.

Contents

GAME PLAN AFTER LOSING JOB

1. Don't panic.
2. Be yourself.
3. Have no regrets.
4. Don't count on friends for help.
5. Get out of the house.
6. Work out—physically hard.
7. Do something you always wanted to do.
8. Plant a seed every day.
9. Ask for advice from someone you respect.
10. Help someone who needs it.
11. Your biggest problem is being negative. Be positive.
12. Do something to improve every day.
13. Be direct. Call for jobs yourself.
14. Keep fighting.
15. Keep reading. ☞

Introduction

It has been said that we're born for pain, that if we don't come into the world crying, the doctor spanks us until we start.

Being a coach is something like being born. It's only a matter of time until the pain starts. You feel it when you lose your first game. But you really feel it when you lose your job—as you almost surely will sooner or later. Sometimes it's sooner than you can believe. One year I was fired before the season even started.

Every day, in every field, people get fired. But in professional sports we become experts at it. Like babies, coaches and managers are born to be bounced.

Why this should be so is an enduring mystery that has confounded even our foremost sports journalists, who have otherwise unfailingly furnished solutions to the great problems besetting humankind. My friend Mel Durslag once explored this mystery in a column about Jim Frey, the baseball manager who not long before had been separated from the service of the Kansas City Royals. Frey had gone to Kansas City to replace Whitey Herzog, whose departure was itself a source of some bewilderment, given that the Royals had won three division championships under his command.

Durslag suggested that a team of specialists in Vienna be commissioned to undertake a clinical study of Herzog's dismissal and that, working with laboratory rats, they seek "to isolate behavioral patterns applicable to people who own baseball clubs."

"One reason given for the uncoupling of Herzog," Durslag wrote, "is that he couldn't beat the Yankees in the playoffs. So the Royals hire Jim Frey, who wins his division by fourteen [games] and flattens the Yankees in three. And before he even can complete the following season, which is confused by a strike and turned into a street league of sorts, they fire Frey. . . . Of course, at the time of his detachment . . . Kansas City was languishing exactly a half game out of the lead."[1]

Without presuming to have unlocked the mystery, I would guess that club owners often fire coaches and managers just to give an illusion of action in the face of a playoff loss or some other perceived crisis. Dismissals may have less to do with quality of performance, as measured objectively by long-term records, than with expediency.

Look at some of the people who have been fired. Sparky Anderson was dismissed by the Cincinnati Reds and Billy Martin by the New York Yankees, though their knowledge of the game and capacity to lead were beyond serious question. Martin, in fact, was fired by the Yankees twice. While that is certainly a distinction, it is not unsurpassed in the professional arena. I don't know who holds the all-time record for "most times fired by one team." But I know it's not Martin. Because the Los Angeles Rams fired guy three times.

Me.

Happily, most people cannot match that record. But millions lose jobs every year. They may be as well known as Lee Iacocca, former chairman of the board of Ford Motor Company; Earl Butz, former secretary of agriculture, or Bert Parks, former master of ceremonies of the Miss America Pageant. They may be as unknown as any of five thousand workers laid off in a cutback at an automobile plant. But all are disemployees.[2] And all are exposed to a common peril. Their sense of failure at being fired, or frustration at being laid off, can be devastating, and may occasionally even lead to suicide.

I know the feeling. I went through firings that could have divided my family, even destroyed our lives—if we'd let them.

You don't have to let them. The problem is beatable in nearly every case. In my own, I learned that a man and his family, sticking together, can not only survive but come through stronger and closer than ever. There was never any real doubt in my mind that I would lick the problem. It was just a matter of devising a new kind of game plan.

One thing bound to help is knowing what feelings will surface and how to handle them. Certain guidelines are useful, if not indispensable. Those guidelines are the game plan that makes up much of this book.

To a degree, the book has been a labor of hate. As a football coach, I was disemployed four times, and recalling those episodes has not been a fond reminiscence. (Nor have I particularly enjoyed recalling those occasions on which, as a general manager, I found it necessary to let people go.) But if I can offer even a few ideas that will help the reader ride out the crisis of unemployment, it will have been worth the discomfort.

As I write this, the crisis spreads. Just a few weeks ago I read that there were nine million people out of work in the United States.

By the time you read this, I hope, the picture will have improved. But whether the economy is surging or sinking, there are always people out of work. This book is for all such people, but especially for those who have appeared as guests of dishonor before the firing squad.

GEORGE ALLEN

Los Angeles
Christmas, 1981

---

1. Melvin Durslag, "It's Too Easy Today to Own a Sports Franchise," *Los Angeles Herald Examiner*, September 4, 1981.

2. A disemployee (in case you share Webster's unfamiliarity with the term) is anyone who has lost a job, whether by dismissal or layoff.

1 / *The Falling of the Axe*

THE FIRST TIME

Thursday, December 26, 1968. The phone rang.

The slightly hoarse voice at the other end belonged to Dan Reeves. He owned the Los Angeles Rams. I was the coach.

Dan was a heavy smoker and always talked as if troubled by a mildly sore throat. But now something else was troubling him, and not just mildly. He got right to the point:

"George, I didn't want to ruin your Christmas, so I waited until today to call you. I'm relieving you as head coach."

Dan was not a screamer. He spoke rather softly. But the words hit me like shrapnel.

"Dan . . . I don't . . . Why?"

"It just hasn't worked out, George. Let's face it: You and I have a personality conflict."

"Dan, couldn't we get together and talk? To see if we could work it out?"

"No, George. My mind is made up."

Coaching ability was not at issue, Reeves said, assuring me that he thought I was a fine coach and that I would have no trouble finding a head coaching job elsewhere. He didn't mention where.

He called about 8 a.m. I remember glancing at the bedside clock. I was already awake and so was my wife, Etty. We were in bed, talking about the nice Christmas we'd had with the kids at our new home on the Palos Verdes Peninsula. Etty could tell something was wrong just from my end of the conversation. She wasn't sure how wrong until I hung up, shook my head and said, "He fired me."

I don't know which of us was more amazed. I had just completed my third season with the Rams. The first was what is known euphemistically as a "rebuilding year." The short of it is that the Rams hadn't had a winning season since the middle of the second Eisenhower administration.

In my first year with the club, we went 8-6. We won 75 percent of our games the next two seasons.

One of my favorite years was 1967. Statistically, it was the best season the Rams ever had. We beat Vince Lombardi's Green Bay Packers in the last minute at Los Angeles, then beat Johnny Unitas and the Baltimore Colts, who had come into the game undefeated. Next we had to beat the Packers again, in a playoff game at Milwaukee. We didn't. But it was still a great season. We played twenty-two games, counting exhibitions, and won eighteen, losing only two and tying two. We scored more points (398) than any other team in the league and allowed the fewest (192).

But that was 1967. Now it was 1968, and Dan Reeves had left a pink slip under my Christmas tree. We'd had another good year on the field, winning ten games, losing three, tying one. At one point we had won fourteen consecutive regular-season games (the streak having begun the year before). It was the third longest streak of its kind in NFL history. Given our record, some found Reeves's Christmas gift hard to explain. But I guess it could have been worse. When Dan called to fire me, he could have made it collect.

My son Bruce, who was then twelve, recalled how it was for the kids that morning: "We were watching TV downstairs. The

"I think we should talk," Dan Reeves said.

I got to his home in Bel Air around noon.

"I'm thinking of bringing you back," he said.

In addition to the prospect of reemployment, he offered me a drink. He had done this before and I had always declined. Apart from having had an occasional glass of blackberry brandy for stomach relaxation, I can't offer much in the way of drinking credentials. But this time I surprised him and drank a Scotch and soda. Not only that, but I asked for a second (though I didn't drink it, having already exceeded my quota by one). Dan got a big kick out of that, and later told the press about it.

We talked about some of our past problems. I said he was sometimes away from the office for days at a time and I couldn't always reach him. One reason was that he was undergoing medical treatment. His health was failing. But decisions still had to be made about team personnel and operations. Sometimes I would make them. He didn't like that. It was, after all, his team. But I said there are times when a decision must be made in a hurry and the team may be hurt if the owner can't be reached to make it.

"I'll be available," Reeves promised.

Bel Air was getting to be one of my favorite neighborhoods. Less than a week after being offered a head coaching job by one of its many illustrious residents (Cooke), I was being offered a head coaching job by another (Reeves). This time I decided to accept, though not everything was settled at that meeting. Reeves called a news conference later to announce my resurrection.

Shortly after being rehired, I gave Dan an annual report, evaluating the performance of our personnel in 1968 and offering a forecast for 1969. I wasn't asked for the report. I just thought it was something the owner should have. It ran ten pages and was signed off, "Your Loving Coach, George Allen."

Reeves, I learned later, loved the ending. "I never knew George Allen had a sense of humor like that," he said. (In pro football, I would later conclude, at least a little sense of humor is essential to the preservation of the rest of your senses.)

Anyway, after a whirlwind estrangement, Dan and I were back together. On the banquet circuit, I used to tell a story about the experience:

"I was fired on Christmas [I fudged by a day for effect] and rehired on New Year's Day, and I'm anxiously awaiting the next major holiday."

In the newspapers, Dan was quoted as saying that my announced desire to finish the job was one reason he brought me back. I later learned that Dan had offered the job to Vince Lombardi shortly after firing me but that Lombardi had turned it down. (Oddly, Lombardi would wind up leaving the Green Bay Packers to take the job I had turned down with the Redskins. Odder yet, I would eventually land in Washington myself, and years later would rejoin the Rams once again—only to be fired again.)

Getting fired is not all bad. For one thing, you get a lot of free time. The trouble is nothing else is free when you're not working. This brings to mind an old line attributed variously to several college football coaches who looked with disfavor on the passing game: "Three things can happen when you throw a forward pass, and two of them are bad."

The forward pass has nonetheless attained considerable popularity, no doubt because the one good thing that can happen (a completion) may in the long run outweigh the two bad things (incompletion and interception). A cost-benefit analysis of getting fired, however, will yield a somewhat less favorable result.

The fact is that getting fired has little more to recommend it than getting arrested. Both experiences may teach you something. Being arrested, for example, teaches that crime does not pay. Alas, the wages are usually no better when a person gets fired. (I say usually because coaches and others with written agreements may have to be paid off for any time remaining on their contracts if they are fired.)

But a person who has had enough experience at it can learn many useful things from being fired. I am such a person. And my main purpose in this book will be to pass along the lessons.

So far, however, we have reviewed only one of my firings in

detail. And I didn't have enough time to learn much from that one. My education was cut short when I was rehired before I really got the hang of being fired.

But further educational opportunities lay ahead. If you doubt I've been fired enough to become a real authority on the subject, read on.

THE SECOND TIME

When I rejoined the Rams after my first firing, I knew the odds were decidedly against my being kept on when my contract ran out in 1970. Had Vince Lombardi been willing to go to Los Angeles, I wouldn't even have been around for the 1969 season. By landing a coach with Lombardi's name, Dan Reeves could have neutralized a lot of the negative reaction to my firing. But he couldn't get Lombardi and was under pressure from fans and players to take me back. I had no illusions. He did not rehire me because ours was a relationship conceived in paradise. He did it because it was a practical short-term solution.

Given our personality differences, it could not have been a long-term solution. Dan was a sociable man who liked coaches with his social inclinations. People he could go out to dinner with, have a few drinks with, talk football with into the night.

I wasn't any of those people. Not that I was a recluse. I've attended my share of off-season banquets and have the indigestion to prove it. In season, though, I never had much time for going out with anyone. Ask my wife.

I learned long ago that I loved coaching more than anything but my family. It was all I wanted to do. Even if I hadn't loved it so much, I think I would have realized I had to give it just about all my waking hours if I hoped to stay ahead of, or even abreast of, the better coaches in the National Football League.

Anyway, I knew when I rejoined the Rams in 1969 that I was working on Pacific Borrowed Time. We won our first eleven games that year, setting a team record, and took the Coastal

Division title. Dan and I probably saw more of each other than we had the year before, but it was still not a close relationship.

I hardly saw Dan at all during the 1970 season (when we finished second in our division with a record of 9-4-1). He then had less than a year to live and, as I remember, was in New York much of the time, receiving medical treatment.

If I needed any confirmation that my contract would not be renewed, I got it late in the 1970 season. A representative of the Houston Oilers came to Los Angeles to offer me a job. We sat in my kitchen. He said the Oilers had Reeves's permission to talk to me. Translation: I would soon be disemployed and available.

The Oilers wanted to bring my whole family to Houston for a visit. But I never made the trip. At the moment, I said, I couldn't give proper consideration to any job offer because the season was still on and the Rams were again in contention.

Shortly after the season, Dan and I talked by phone for the last time. He was in New York.

"George," he said, "I think I'm going to let your contract run out and not renew it."

It was one of the milder surprises of my career. I didn't even bother asking why he wouldn't bring me back. I knew. Dan Reeves and George Allen would never be on the same page.

To my mind, this firing was no more justified than the first. In my five years in Los Angeles, the Rams had won forty-nine games, lost seventeen and tied four. But whether you deserve it or not, getting fired is being told you failed. Even if you know you didn't fail, there are those who will believe that in some way you must have. Or you wouldn't have been fired.

But apart from the embarrassment that goes with it, I honestly never worried about losing my job. I always did what I knew would help my team win. If you worry constantly about your job, you'll be distracted, and probably start making mistakes, and probably get fired. If I'm going to be fired, I'd rather spend my remaining time running things my way than running scared. Some coaches allow themselves to be turned into puppets. I'd rather be George Allen, with no strings attached. You have to run a team with confidence and conviction, or you'll run it into the ground. I followed my convictions because I knew from experience that they would produce success. And I told myself that if I lost one job the next one would be better.

That's the way it worked out when I left the Rams after the 1970 season. I had not one job offer but five, counting the one from Houston late in the season. The others were from the Washington Redskins, Green Bay Packers, Buffalo Bills and Philadelphia Eagles.

I took the Washington job. It was not the most appealing financially, but I decided to go with the Redskins because Jack Kent Cooke was a friend and Washington would be an exciting place to live. Also, the Redskins had the makings of a good offense. Their defense was atrocious, about the worst in the league. But I knew we could straighten that out.

So Los Angeles was behind me (for the time being). I didn't take any parting shots at the Ram organization, and I won't take any now. It's tempting, when you've been through the ordeal of a dismissal, to get out your side of the story. But what one man sees as sweet revenge may strike another as sour grapes. I thought Dan Reeves made a mistake when he let me go, both times. But I'm just as sure he thought he was doing the right thing.

Dan died in April 1971 of Hodgkin's disease. He had many friends. He was a decent man.

THE THIRD TIME

I was in Washington seven years, almost the equivalent of two presidential terms, and couldn't have enjoyed myself more if my address had been 1600 Pennsylvania Avenue. Edward Bennett Williams, the man I had to answer to, probably would tell you that I'd have spent less money running the country than I did running our office and training facility at Redskin Park. You may remember the crack Williams made not long after I took over as general manager and head coach: "I gave George Allen an unlimited budget, and he's already exceeded it."

But there have been worse investments. In seven years, we made the playoffs five times, the Super Bowl once. I loved the team, the fans, the area. Those were the happiest years of my life. The only thing I didn't like about Washington was leaving it.

The high point of my time there was on January 1, 1973, when we defeated the Dallas Cowboys, 26-3, in the National Conference title game. The Cowboys were defending NFL champions, and that game seemed to do much to bring the city together. I saw blacks and whites hugging and kissing. Even Republicans and Democrats, of all people, agreed that the team was helping heal the civic sores exposed by the race riots of 1970. The family and I attended a New Year's party at the Shoreham Hotel, and I led the band in an exuberant rendition of "California, Here I Come." We were going to the Super Bowl.

We lost to the Miami Dolphins, 14-7. But worse moments than that lay ahead.

My contract was up after the seventh season, and the Redskins offered me a new five-year deal. It was a good one. But there was a disagreement over whether I should retain an option I had in my original contract. It gave me the right to buy 5 percent of the franchise. I wanted the option extended. They didn't.

Ed Williams waited for my response to the new contract offer. I kept putting him off. He got tired of waiting, and said so. His patience was being tested. It apparently flunked the test. I was fired.

I think Williams suspected I might beat him to the punch by resigning. In fact, I had decided to accept his last offer and forget about the option. But I hadn't gotten around to telling him of my decision. I'll have to admit that was a rather serious oversight.

It was a shame. We had accomplished so much in seven years. I had hoped to finish my coaching career in Washington. And, until the late going, Williams had shared that hope. Or so he indicated. He had said George Allen would be the last coach he would hire. He had been proud to be president of the Redskins since Allen took over. He wanted me to stay and keep the team winning. That was five months before he fired me.

In retrospect, I must admit I made a mistake letting that job go, just as I thought the Rams had when they let me go.

THE FOURTH TIME

This was the strangest one of all.

In 1978, the Rams hired me as head coach for the third time. That sounds strange enough in itself. You could just about count on the fingers of one foot the number of coaches hired three times by the same team. But it gets curiouser yet.

We lost our first two exhibition games, the second on a Saturday night. Sunday morning, general manager Don Klosterman called and said Carroll Rosenbloom, the club president, was coming to see me at training camp. On the face of it, there was nothing unusual about that. Carroll often paid such visits.

He arrived about three in the afternoon. Carroll, his son, Steve, and Klosterman came to my room in a dormitory at Cal State Fullerton, some twenty-five miles southeast of Los Angeles. Carroll sat down and began questioning me about the team. Did I think we could win with Pat Haden at quarterback? (The answer was yes.) We went over other personnel, talking for maybe a half hour or forty-five minutes. Then, without warning: "George, why don't you take a leave of absence, for your health?"

There was a pause. I was stunned.

"Carroll," I said finally, "there's nothing wrong with my health, and the last thing I'm going to do is take a leave of absence."

I wanted to change the subject. But Rosenbloom wouldn't let it drop.

"Carroll," I said, "things are shaping up. This is going to be a championship football team. That loss last night means nothing. Absolutely nothing."

My assurance meant about the same thing. Rosenbloom said he thought he should make a coaching change.

"Carroll," I said, "you made a correct decision when you brought me here, and now you're making a mistake. And I guess I made a mistake coming, because I gave up a pretty good job in Washington."

Carroll was unimpressed by my argument. I dropped it.

I didn't want to leave the players and assistant coaches without saying goodbye, so I called them together and told them the season was ending for me before it began.

Klosterman later told me I should have given Carroll more of an argument. "If you'd talked some more," Don said, "you could have saved your job. You could have talked him out of it."

I said I didn't feel like trying to talk him out of it. If things could go that wrong that easily that early, I said, it meant certain trouble ahead.

There was talk that I had been behaving strangely, and that may have been what Carroll was alluding to when he suggested a leave of absence for my "health." Well, I don't deny I'm eccentric in some ways. My approach to work, for example, strikes some as obsessive. But I was no more eccentric in 1978 than I was coaching high school football twenty-five years earlier.

An example of my supposedly strange behavior, I heard later, was that I had been fussing because players getting soup at one end of the serving line in the team cafeteria had to go clear to the other end to get crackers.

It was a small thing to fuss about. But I didn't try to make it a big thing. I simply said the crackers were in the wrong place. And they were. I happen to believe in order. I also happen to believe that small problems, if allowed to accumulate, can ripen into big problems.

I'll let it go at that. I don't want to be accused of making a late hit on Carroll. He drowned while swimming in Florida in 1979. He was in his seventies, but still too young to die. He had enough energy and enthusiasm to supply two men half his age.

Actually, in the end, Carroll and I were in agreement. About ten days before his death, he called me at home and we talked for a half hour or more. He said he sometimes woke up in the middle of the night, thinking about how he'd let me go. He said it was a mistake.

That didn't undo my dismissal. I was still a four-time loser. Nonetheless, I had put in twelve years as an NFL head coach and had a pretty good report card. To be sure, there were four final grades of F (for Fired), but they seemed to be contradicted by the numbers. Have a look at the record.

Of all my firings, the last was the hardest to take. First, I had no inkling. Second, it was so utterly frustrating, being let go before the regular season even started. I still can't figure it out. It's like being promised a big movie part and then being told just before shooting starts that you are to be found dead in the opening scene.

I still have a memento of my cameo appearance with the Rams that year. One day I found a neatly wrapped bottle of blackberry brandy on my desk. There was a note from Johnny Sanders, a Ram staff member who would later become general manager of the San Diego Chargers. Johnny wrote that he was sure I'd have a long and successful tour of duty.

A week later I was gone. I still have the bottle, unopened. I want something connected with that job to last.

Many people take to the bottle after losing jobs. It's a discredited cure for unemployment. I think I've learned at least part of the formula for a real cure. Instead of bottling it, I've decided to write it. And you're invited to read it.

GEORGE ALLEN'S NFL COACHING RECORD

	Won	Lost	Tied	%	Points Scored	Points Allowed	Finish in Division
Rams							
1966	8	6	0	.571	289	212	3rd*
1967	11	1	2	.857	398	196	1st†‡
1968	10	3	1	.750	312	200	2nd

[Fired and rehired between seasons]

1969	11	3	0	.785	320	243	1st†
1970	9	4	1	.679	325	202	2nd

[Fired after season]

	Won	Lost	Tied	%	Points Scored	Points Allowed	Finish in Division
Redskins							
1971	9	4	1	.679	276	190	2nd†§
1972	11	3	0	.785	336	218	1st†‖
1973	10	4	0	.714	325	198	1st†#
1974	10	4	0	.714	320	196	1st†#
1975	8	6	0	.571	325	276	3rd
1976	10	4	0	.714	291	217	2nd†
1977	9	5	0	.643	196	189	2nd

[Fired after season]

	Won	Lost	Tied	%	Points Scored	Points Allowed	Finish in Division
Rams							
1978	0	0	0	.000	—	—	—

[Fired before regular season]

	Won	Lost	Tied	%	Points Scored	Points Allowed	Finish in Division
Totals	116	47	5**	.705††	3,713‡‡	2,537‡‡	—

* Divisions created in 1967; Rams third in seven-team Western Conference in 1966.
† Qualified for playoffs.
‡ Los Angeles in playoffs for first time in 12 years.
§ Washington in playoffs for first time in 26 years.
‖ Won Eastern Division and National Conference championships, Washington's first titles in 30 years.
Tied for first.
** Each tie is counted as ½ game won and ½ game lost in computing won-lost percentage.
†† Won average of 7 games in 10.
‡‡ Scored 46% more points than opponents.

2 / *How to React*

TWO DON'TS

A person who has just been fired is apt to face at least two temptations. One is to strike back, to give the boss an earful. Another, arising from a sense of shame, is to go into hiding.

Don't do either.

First reactions to being fired vary widely. The victims may argue, curse, cry, collapse, plead for mercy, call their lawyers or all of the above. Or they may simply be struck dumb.

Fired employees have on occasion threatened to kill their bosses, have sabotaged company equipment, have turned on themselves and committed suicide. While most do not go to any of these extremes, the fact that such reactions are known demonstrates the potential volatility of the situation.

Your boss, Hiram Firem, has just given you the word. Stunned, you stand there, staring. Then you start groping for words. You finally find one: "Me?"

"I'm afraid so," Firem says. "Of course, you'll get your severance and . . ."

You miss most of the rest of it. Panic scrambles all incoming signals. But you struggle to focus your mind and are at least dimly aware when Firem leaves you with a parting thought: "I'm sorry, but that's the way it is."

The authenticity of his sorrow is open to question, but you're still fired. Now that it's over, why not give the old buzzard a piece of your tormented mind? You might even be doing him a favor by wising him up, telling him a few things he didn't know about himself. But you might also antagonize him to the point that he would go out of his way to put in a bad word for you at the next opportunity. Remember, you'll have to say what your last job was when you apply for your next one, and your prospective employer may contact Hiram Firem. At best, that probably would not be a favorable prospect. No point in making it worse—in turning what could be only a somewhat negative reference into one that could wipe out your next job opportunity.

Another reason to restrain yourself is that exploding may brand you as a hothead. An explosion may be entirely justified, but how do you know it will sound that way when the story reaches a prospective employer? The facts may have been somewhat distorted by then, and you could come off looking less like a mistreated employee than a malcontent.

Yet another argument against letting out your anger is that you could get carried away and say things you don't really mean. You could even be tempted to take physical reprisal. It happens. The following is just one of many stories that could be used to illustrate the point:

> BIRMINGHAM, Ala. (AP)—Rep. Albert Lee Smith Jr. (R-Ala.) says he is disappointed in an aide who punched him in the mouth after the congressman fired him in a dispute over a minority jobs program.
>
> Smith said the blow made him fall backward on a marble staircase at the federal courthouse Saturday night. He was treated briefly at a hospital. . . .
>
> Lige Richardson, who admitted punching Smith, and Peter Gresham, another fired aide, were arrested and held about two hours. . . .
>
> Smith said he would ask the U.S. attorney's office not to press charges.[1]

The next person to punch an ex-boss may not get off that easily. In any event, losing your self-control is always harmful—

to you if to no one else. It may take prodigious willpower to control yourself, but nothing good will come of working yourself into a rage. It's childish.

Bear in mind also that there is such a thing as triumph in tragedy. While losing a job is not as traumatic as losing a loved one, people expect you to go to pieces. This is why employers often avoid direct confrontation in the dismissal process and either have someone else deliver the message or give the unlucky employee written notice. Almost no one wants to watch a person fall apart. It's an unsavory scene, embarrassing on both sides.

You can turn the situation to your advantage through self-discipline. People will admire your character if you keep your composure. Reacting calmly will also give you the satisfaction of disappointing anyone who was hoping to watch your wheels come off.

I know how painful dismissal can be. But try to act as if you're quite prepared to deal with it. The idea is not to pretend that nothing has gone wrong but to show that you can take adversity in stride.

It is unlikely that Firem decided to fire you on the spur of the moment, or that he can now be talked out of it. So when there is really nothing left to say, say it. Shake hands with Firem (taking care not to crush his fingers) and leave gracefully. Courage, as the saying goes, is grace under pressure.

If you're fired at work, don't stop to talk to anyone. Company gossips may want a firsthand account of what happened. Leave them unsatisfied. Your emotional state makes this absolutely the wrong time to discuss the matter.

If your firing is not effective immediately, try to use your remaining time on the job to your advantage. Your attitude and work habits should be exemplary. Remember, the past is hardened concrete, and your task now is to build a new foundation for the future.

The short of it is to save your anger for your memoirs.

The second temptation—to go into hiding—may be even harder to resist. The natural inclination is to go underground, to avoid having to face people as a certified failure.

Defeating this impulse is imperative. Think of yourself as a boxer. Your image will suffer if you get knocked down, but you can recover a lot of that lost esteem, and maybe even win new respect, by struggling to your feet and plunging back into the fight.

It's not easy to get back in the fight when you're still stunned and hurting. I've been there. Before I was fired by the Rams the last time, I accepted an invitation to a Friars' Club roast for Howard Cosell at the Beverly Wilshire Hotel in Beverly Hills. After my firing, I decided not to go. Then I decided I should. I guess I must have changed my mind at least five times. Finally I headed up the freeway with Bob Reis, a friend who offered to drive me to the hotel. Several times I almost told Bob to turn around and take me home. I kept thinking that going to that dinner meant certain embarrassment. When we reached the hotel, I had to force myself out of the car. Here I was, in one of the lowest periods of my life, showing up for an evening of frivolity. I felt as out of place as a tailor in a nudist colony.

Among the celebrities on hand were Milton Berle, George Jessel, Phil Silvers, Telly Savalas and Ray Bolger. Ordinarily, in such company, I would have anticipated a most enjoyable evening. This wasn't ordinarily.

But I had a surprise coming. The evening was a great success, for me as well as for Howard Cosell. When I was introduced, I got a standing ovation that must have lasted two minutes. I don't think anybody expected me to show up. Milton Berle, the emcee, didn't call on me to speak. He said I should just sit back and enjoy myself. I did. I relaxed for the first time in days.

During his closing remarks, Howard looked to my end of the dais and said, "There is one man here tonight who has as much character and guts as anyone I know, and he is coach George Allen."

That meant a lot to me. People take a lot of shots at Howard. But I consider him a friend. He is articulate, outspoken, honest. And what he said that night really helped me. It made me realize there were people out there who still cared about me, still believed in me.

I'm not suggesting that anyone who is fired will get a standing ovation every time he leaves his house. But I think that by getting out and mixing with people, visiting friends and acquaintances, you'll find that you're not as alone as you thought. Some of your friends will have gone through the same ordeal, and will be able to offer advice. Everyone will admire you for confronting your crisis.

It does take courage. You don't want to go anywhere. You don't even want to take phone calls. You want to be alone.

And you should be, some of the time. You'll need that time to organize your thinking, recharge your batteries. But there is no point in trying to hide from the world indefinitely. If you do, there will soon be no reason to hide, because no one will be looking for you.

You get the idea: The postfiring period is not a time to hide but a time to seek. Staying out of sight is a good way to stay out of work. As someone put it, you should not wait for the phone to ring; you should make it ring.

BREAKING THE NEWS

If you've been disemployed as many times as I have, it becomes hard to recall specific reactions, to separate the events of one firing from those of another. They tend to run together.

But I know this: Of the four times I lost jobs, easily the most painful was the last time, when the Rams released me in the middle of the 1978 exhibition season. After Carroll Rosenbloom gave me the news, I sat in my office at training camp, wondering how I should go about telling Etty and the kids.

I knew the story would soon be on the news wires and television, and I wanted the family to know first. Despite my best efforts, it didn't turn out that way.

But I did get to my wife first. She liked to kid me about not being home enough, having so many meetings and working long hours. I told her, "I have some good news for you. I'll be home early tonight."

"Well, the house is a mess," she said. "The movers are unloading furniture [just arrived from our old home near Washington], and a second truckload is coming tomorrow." I told her not to worry about it.

"I want to tell you one more thing," I said. "I'm coming home to stay."

She asked what I meant, and I told her I'd just been fired again. She didn't say anything. I thought she might have fainted. I hung up and called back. I had to do it several times before she answered. When I finally got her, she said, "You're not kidding, are you? Don't kid about something like this."

"I'm not kidding," I said. "Carroll just fired me, and I wanted you to know about it before it hit the news media." I asked her to get in touch with the kids while I was on the way home. She tried, but all except George had heard the news from other sources before she could get to them. (She reached George at the University of Virginia. Bruce was at Arizona State. He attended a banquet that evening and overheard two people at an adjoining table discussing the firing. He called Jennifer and told her. Gregory was on his way to San Diego when he heard the news on his car radio. He turned around and drove back home.)

From living through it and having thought it through—more than once—I've concluded that several rules should be followed in breaking the news to the family.

First, be strong. Try to sound like the same person you were before the firing. Don't come crawling home like a whipped dog. You could drag down the morale of the whole family. This does not mean you should understate the gravity of the situation. If the firing will necessitate an immediate cutback in family spending, say so. If not, offer that reassurance. Don't mislead the family in either direction. If you do, your deception will probably be exposed before long, and will not be appreciated.

Stay calm. Or at least try to look calm. Somehow, you should get this message across to the family: "Don't panic. We're going to make it. If we stick together, we can survive anything."

In recent years, many authorities have written about the disintegration of the American family. I won't challenge their findings except to say that in times of crisis the family can still pull together with remarkable effectiveness. At such times, you will need your family as much as it needs you. You should express confidence, but don't try to carry the burden for the entire family. You probably couldn't if you wanted to. The firing is likely to affect the family almost as much as it does you.

Take our daughter, Jennifer. She was a high school senior when I left the Redskins. We brought her along when we moved back to our home on the Palos Verdes Peninsula after the Rams rehired me. She had to give up cheerleading and other activities to make the move. She had made many friends in Washington and had none in California. These considerations alone probably would have been enough to ruin her senior year. If not, her father's firing clinched it. She became depressed and started giving away clothes, mementos and other belongings. Sometimes, Etty said, Jennifer would go to her room and cry after coming home from school.

We probably made a mistake bringing Jennifer back to California. We could have let her finish her senior year in the Washington area and graduate there. We had friends she could have stayed with. It simply never occurred to us how much the move would disrupt her life. And of course we could not foresee how much that disruption would be compounded by my firing. It really hit her. I was the one who lost the job, but her loss seemed just as great.

A parent out of work can make matters worse for the whole family by hitting the panic button. I'm reminded somehow of a scene that seemed to turn up repeatedly in those old grade-B westerns. The hero or his faithful sidekick would get winged in the film's climactic gunfight. Clutching a bleeding shoulder and forcing a faint smile, he would assure his partner, "It's only a flesh wound."

The idea, of course, was to conceal the pain. It was, admittedly, a corny scene, and yet perhaps worthy of imitation by the father or mother who has just lost a job. As family leaders, parents are responsible for preserving the household's esprit de corps. A display of character in time of crisis is bound to have a positive influence on the rest of the family. Both parents can contribute.

My wife was a great stabilizing influence in our household whenever I had just been fired, and she is not the only coach's wife entitled to a citation for valor. As this was written, hockey coach Don Cherry had been fired three times (most recently by the Colorado Rockies). He was not sure he could have survived without his wife.

In a letter, Cherry told me an amusing story about one of his dismissals: "I got fired once by a [general] manager who said, 'Well done . . . We are going to make a change in your department.' I was thinking, Gosh, who is in my department? Then I realized I was the only one."

Cherry got word of his last dismissal from a reporter. That surprised him. "I thought I would be told in person and not hear it through the press," he said. "I was with my wife, Rose, who is a rock in these situations. I had been through this twice before, and I really don't know how I would have made out if my wife had not stood beside me, even though she thought I was wrong on some things. . . .

"When a person is fired—and I had a tough firing—it is very important that he has a strong family [that] gives confidence with no wailing and weeping. Because, [above] all else, the person must keep his confidence."

Fired husbands also have acquitted themselves in exemplary fashion, as illustrated by an article in *Woman's Day:*

"When George Jackson lost his job as a chain-store manager during a company-wide layoff in the spring of 1979, his subsequent six-month period of unemployment could have been devastating for George and his family—but it wasn't.

"For one thing, Helen, George's wife, and their three children . . . were all producing some income on their own. . . . But more important than the money they were earning was their positive and mutually supportive attitude. It was their team approach to the crisis that helped them not only weather unemployment but emerge stronger for it. . . .

" 'It was a very worrisome time, but situations like this *are* character builders,' Helen says now. . . . 'The more time that passed, the harder it got, but George kept going. He spent at least twenty hours a week on job hunting. . . . He worked on the yard and kept up his activities with the kids. He didn't let himself dwell on the problem.'

"Helen feels that George's grace under pressure set an example for the rest of the family. Although their standard of living was drastically reduced, no one complained."

Conversely, the article said, a marriage may be threatened if the husband is not only unemployed but unmotivated:

"Sharon Gordon, whose fifty-year-old husband, Carl, has lost several jobs in automotive engineering since the economy began to decline and has been unemployed for almost a year, says that she is now considering a divorce. . . .

"Conjecturing that Carl was let go the last time simply because he didn't get along with his boss, Sharon seems unable to comprehend why her husband is having difficulty finding and keeping a job. 'The worst effect of Carl's unemployment on me personally has been my anger and resentment,' she says. 'It became apparent to me after the first time he lost his job that he didn't put too much effort into looking for work. I kept after him to do more to find a job. I resented his sleeping until noon and then lying around reading all day.' "[2]

Sharon should have been married to someone like Charles Darrow of Germantown, Pennsylvania. In 1934, at the height of the Great Depression, Darrow invented what would become the world's most popular board game: Monopoly. At first he produced the game sets on his own, but the demand was such that he couldn't keep up. So he sold the game to Parker Brothers. And how did he come to invent Monopoly?

"Like a lot of other people, he happened to be unemployed, and he made up the game because he had nothing else to do."[3]

It is of course wildly improbable that you will match Charles

Darrow's masterpiece just by spending a lot of time in creative thought while out of work. A concept like that takes more than time. But it's still a good idea to keep busy. If you can't come up with another Monopoly, you can at least avoid monotony.

PREPARING FOR THE WORST

Let's say you've carried off the first scene with a flourish. Like George Jackson, you've lost your job but not your confidence. And you've persuaded the family it really is only a flesh wound.

This, unfortunately, is only the first round of what could be a long fight. As I mentioned in the Introduction, a recent report showed nine million Americans were out of work. Reflect a moment on that number. That's more people than there are in New York City.

I can see an opportunity here for a graphic illustration of our unemployment problem. It would be a film dramatization. The camera would take us through Manhattan, then the Bronx, then the other boroughs. The streets would be practically deserted, the stores all closed, the skyscrapers empty, the subways shut down, the theaters shuttered, the corner pretzel vendors gone. We would follow the camera through every section of the city and find not a single person working, not a solitary cab in sight.

Unemployment, of course, never hits that hard in one place. But maybe a film like that would help give people a better idea of what the number nine million means.

As matters stand, some of those nine million unemployed could wait a year, perhaps longer, before landing new jobs. George Jackson did better than that. Maybe you'll do even better than he did if you're out of a job. Maybe you won't.

While you should not lose confidence, prudence dictates that you prepare for the worst. You're not giving up. You're just facing the reality that a job will not necessarily turn up before next month's bills come due.

You should assess your resources and lead the family in a

candid discussion of the situation. The discussion need not be morbid. You should talk in calm, reasoned, positive terms, but frankly. If the family faces an authentic crisis, you should say so.

You should go over your financial reserves (e.g., savings accounts, stocks and bonds, insurance policies) and calculate how long you can hold out assuming the worst. In the usual case it should not be necessary for family members to go to such extremes as selling personal effects. Economizing and good judgment are called for, not a blind rush to sell everything in the house.

I found some good suggestions in the *Woman's Day* article quoted a few paragraphs back:

"For many people the sudden loss of income when a breadwinner becomes unemployed has the impact of a torpedo that has rammed the family ship. Unemployment insurance may keep the ship from sinking, but it's rarely enough to eliminate the need for some serious belt tightening. . . . Attitude can make the difference between hard times and havoc.

" 'If you take a good look at what you were doing with your money, you might find a lot more imaginative ways to spend less of it,' says Tillie Speck, manager of the professional and commercial office of the Job Service in Philadelphia. 'People who work don't have a great deal of time to spend cooking and fussing. If you have more time, you can buy cheaper cuts of meat and cook them longer. You can eliminate convenience foods and plan your meals to avoid impulse buying. If you're handy with a needle, you can sew your own clothes or knit a sweater for the winter—something men can do as well as women. Instead of going out for your entertainment, you can invite friends in.' "

The article offered this example of "inventive economizing":

"Maria Steffano found that facial tissue, paper towels and paper napkins were expendable while her husband, Vince, was unemployed; and the family seldom uses them now that Vince has returned to work. 'We have tissues for colds,' says Maria, 'but we still use only terry-cloth hand towels in the kitchen and napkins that don't need ironing.' "

Children should not be shielded from the facts of life when belt tightening is necessary, the article said.

"Although children are generally vulnerable to peer pressure and don't want to be known as the 'poor kids on the block,' most will willingly go along with an austerity program if they are made aware of the reasons for it. When parents mistakenly try to protect their children by concealing the truth about the family's financial difficulties during an unemployment crisis, they only disturb the children more and inhibit their cooperation."

On this score, the article offered a word from psychiatrist Martin Goldberg:

"What children don't know can be more harmful than what they are told. Children always sense when something's wrong, and if it's not spelled out for them, or if an attempt is made to cover it up, they may imagine something much worse than what is actually happening."

Goldberg said families stick together better when they have "transcending values," when they face extraordinary circumstances and are working toward a necessary objective. Economic survival, of course, is such an objective.[4]

Assuming your spouse and children do not already have jobs, one of the first suggestions likely to come up in the family discussion is that they go to work to help out. The suggestion should not be dismissed out of hand.

For the children, getting jobs could be an instructive experience. Contributing to the family's support would give them a sense of responsibility and accomplishment. In the past they may have spent their allowances (or paychecks when working) on clothes and record albums. Now they may have an opportunity to play a more meaningful role in the family economy by getting part-time jobs.

Part-time work may also be a stopgap solution for the out-of-work parent. The need for part-timers apparently is growing. I recently came across these striking statistics:

Seventeen million Americans currently work fewer than thirty-five hours a week, and another four million "moonlight" in part-time jobs.

For the past ten years the number of part-timers has grown more rapidly than the general work force in this country. . . . Society is changing its ideas about work; economic factors, technical developments and sociological shifts, such as the large number of women who are entering the work force, all are making part-time work not only a possible alternative but for many employers a desirable one.[5]

That was written for people who already have jobs and would like to shorten their work weeks. These people apparently are filling many of the openings for part-timers. But it's still an area worth exploring if you're out of work.

Next question: When a man has lost a job, should his wife work? Though millions of women do, some husbands cling to the notion that the man should be the breadwinner and the woman the homemaker. Today, of course, it is a widely discredited notion. My own view is that pride should never stand in the way of the family's welfare. It seems to me to fly in the face of reason to deny other family members an opportunity to help support the family while the husband is job hunting. Whatever his notions about sex roles, he's dealing with an emergency and should do all he can to ease the family's burden. To do otherwise is foolish and self-destructive. When the crisis has passed, the old roles can be reclaimed (assuming, of course, that the wife acquiesces).

In the *Woman's Day* article mentioned previously, the author told of a man who adjusted nicely to a role reversal and a wife who made the adjustment easier:

"Joe Walters, a man in his forties who was forced out of his job in the recession, describes himself as 'a very traditional kind of guy in the past, a guy who pretty much never lifted a finger at home.' But now, while his wife, Betty, is . . . bringing in a fairly decent income as a real estate agent, Joe prepares dinner, vacuums, scrubs the floors, chauffeurs their three teenage children around and still has time to look for another job. His reaction is, 'Hey, it's not all that bad, and I don't feel like dead weight.'

"Unlike other couples who may not interact sexually at all for a significant portion of the unemployment period because of the husband's feelings of inadequacy or depression, Joe and Betty are making love with as much frequency as before—and perhaps even more rewardingly. Betty explained why: 'It's a way of telling Joe that despite the temporary setback of his unemployment, we can enjoy each other. It's my way of saying, "I still love you. I care for you and know you care for me, and we'll pull through this *together*." ' "

But don't expect even a very intelligent woman to bail out her unemployed husband by landing a $50,000-a-year job if she has spent the last ten or twenty years at home. She will probably find getting a good job is even harder work than homemaking. A writer who researched the problem passed along these observations:

"The housewife-mother is often told she's doing the most important job in America: raising the next generation and maintaining family life. But what happens when a woman goes out looking for paid work . . . ? She finds that, despite her worth, employers consider her valueless. . . .

"For many homemakers . . . the experience is nothing short of humiliating. Such was the case with Regina English when she pounded the pavement after twenty years at home as a wife and mother of two. 'No one was looking for a great mommy,' she says. 'Some said I wasn't qualified for anything because I couldn't type. Others said I was overqualified because it would be too "difficult" for me to have someone fresh out of college giving me orders.' After two and a half years . . . English finally landed a public-relations position. She looks back on that period as 'a cruel ordeal.' . . .

"One way to avoid the 'no prospects' dilemma is to begin paving the way before you're actually ready for a full-time job commitment. Market researcher Fay Ennis says free-lancing was her salvation during the six years she stayed home with her twins. Several projects a year kept her sharp and in touch with professional contacts until she resumed full-time work."[6]

Working at home may sound like a good idea to a woman whose husband has just lost his job. It may be especially appealing if the woman has no recent job experience and sees a work-at-home ad saying "Absolutely no experience necessary." Some such jobs may prove profitable. But I should pass along a warning:

"By placing advertisements in newspapers and magazines, work-at-home companies tempt readers with offers of quick money for stuffing envelopes, sewing aprons and investing in 'foolproof' get-rich-quick schemes. (These companies should not be confused with the reputable cosmetics and housewares firms that hire people to sell their products door to door or at home parties.) The potential 'employee' or 'investor' is asked to send a membership or registration fee for further information and for the materials necessary to begin the job. Too often . . . these job materials and investment 'secrets' turn out to be just more promotional literature, not work."[7]

The warning said a work-at-home advertiser may carry the scheme a dangerous step further:

"The consumer is told to place her own advertisement—similar to the original one—in the paper, inducing others to send *her* money for work assignments or investment advice. Not only is it very difficult for the consumer to make a profit, but her advertisement continues to promote the fraud."

An "easy-money" ad may have the ring of salvation to it in time of unemployment. My advice: Forget it.

But there is one readily accessible source of "easy money" that should not be overlooked. Don't let a sense of shame keep you from registering for unemployment compensation. While working, you contributed to the fund from which benefits are paid. It's as though you had been paying insurance premiums and now the time has come to start collecting on the policy. If you need the money, take it. That's what it's there for.

If you don't live on a budget, by all means start doing so at once. You should be able to account for every dollar coming in and going out. If you already have a budget, revise it. Many expenditures can probably be eliminated or sharply reduced. But don't get dramatic and go overboard. If the family is accustomed to going out to dinner once a week, try making it once every two weeks or once a month before cutting it out altogether. It's good to have pleasurable family experiences like that to look forward to.

On the other hand, don't cling to luxuries when sound budgetary considerations call for their elimination. It's easy to persuade yourself of the absolute necessity of taking that annual trip to Europe "to restore the spirit," or of hanging on to your boat or plane or ski cabin no matter what. Clinging to such things on the grounds that they are essential to the health of the soul may sound rational in a mystical sort of way. It's also an easy way to think. Avoid easy thinking. When you're out of work it's time for hard thinking.

Take your bills. You should go over them carefully and group them by priorities. Some creditors, including the telephone company, electric company and landlord, insist on being paid in full every month. Other bills may require only partial payments; Sears, MasterCard and Visa are examples. The minimum-payment option can be a lifesaver, even though you have to pay for it eventually in interest charges.

Let's say your spouse has a job and two of the children are working but the family still doesn't have enough income to meet obligations as they come due.

Dipping into your savings account (assuming you have one) is an obvious move. Selling stocks and bonds is another. Cashing in some or all of your life-insurance policies is a third. This is a drastic measure and should not be a first option for obvious reasons. But you may not be able to keep paying your premiums while unemployed. Talk to your insurance agent. His company doesn't want to lose your business. And he doesn't want to lose the commission he gets on your policy. You may be able to have your payments deferred for at least a short period (usually only thirty days).

Another alternative may be to borrow money from the insurance company, using your policy as collateral. Insurance company interest rates are comparatively low. But since you will be borrowing against money you've already paid in, it's not all that terrific a bargain. In effect, you're paying the company twice, once in premiums and once in interest on your loan. Still, it would be unfair to call it a ripoff. It could be a sensible way out in an emergency.

Do not, under any circumstances, reduce or cancel hospitalization insurance on yourself or other family members. Even a brief stay in the hospital can wipe out life savings if a family is uninsured. If you lost all your hospitalization insurance with your job, you should seriously consider buying at least some new protection, even if it will strain your budget.

What if you own real estate in addition to your home? Should you sell?

I'm told there are two times (and only two) when you should consider selling real estate: (1) when you can get a really handsome price for it, and (2) when you can't afford to keep it.

If you think the answer is (2), review your budget and consider any available alternatives before selling. Land is unique and, if well situated, is one of the better investments going. The reason, as Will Rogers wryly observed, is that "They ain't making any more of it."

What if your only real property is your home? Before selling, consider taking out another mortgage and picking up some cash without giving up title to the house.

If you own a vacation home in addition to your principal residence, you might consider selling the spare place. But, again, real property is a solid asset most anywhere in the country, and before selling any of it I would make sure I had no disposable personal property. Say you own two cars. Consider selling one. If you fish, you may own a boat, a trailer, an outboard motor. Consider (painfully) selling them all, unless you would have to do it at distress prices and would practically be giving them away.

Garage sales can perform useful functions. They make money and give you a chance to get rid of a lot of junk you probably haven't used in years and will never need. If you've never attended a garage sale, you may be amazed to hear what people will buy at one: empty television cabinets, one-legged chairs, two-legged tables, transistor radios with tags certifying that they are inoperative, and even uninflatable balloons.

You may also find willing buyers for sporting equipment, old phonograph records and tapes, musical instruments, toys, books, curtains, towels, automobile accessories, vases, planters, garden tools, costume jewelry, ashtrays, picture frames, eyeglasses, toiletries, kitchen utensils, drinking glasses, tableware, electrical appliances. If the price is right, people will buy practically anything you own—with one notable exception: clothing. Garage-sale veterans say many people who would not hesitate to snap up rusty bicycles or cracked dishes are embarrassed at the thought of buying secondhand clothing. Experts usually go light on the clothes and save most of their space for the real "junque."

Even if a garage sale won't cure your financial problems, it will serve a beneficial purpose by keeping you busy for a day or two. Forcing yourself to keep busy is sometimes a good idea when you've got nothing to do. For instance, when you're out of work.

But don't put the garage sale at the head of your list of financial maneuvers. That spot should be reserved for a far more important item: your budget.

If you've never organized one, you can put some of your newly found spare time to good use by taking a complete economic inventory and seeing what sort of plan you can come up with. If you have absolutely no idea of how to go about it, head for a good book store and ask the clerk to show you some of the best-sellers in the field.[8] Any one will be worth fitting into your budget. If you're hopelessly torn between two of them, buy both. This is a good time to splurge.

1. "Punch in the Mouth Is Forgiven," *Los Angeles Times,* February 2, 1981.
2. Maxine Schnall, "How to Weather Unemployment," *Woman's Day,* October 14, 1980.
3. "Board Games Kids Liked Best," *Consumer Reports,* November 1981.
4. Maxine Schnall, "How to Weather Unemployment."
5. Beryl Lieff Benderly, "How to Turn the Full-Time Job You Have Into the Part-Time Job You Want," *Redbook,* November 1980.
6. Letty Cottin Pogrebin, "The Working Woman: Looking for a Job? Making Your Homemaker Years Pay Off," *Ladies' Home Journal,* January 1981.
7. Nina Riccio, "Work-at-Home Warning," *McCall's Monthly Newsletter for Women,* February 1981.
8. For example, *Sylvia Porter's Money Book for the 80s* (New York: Avon Books, 1980).

3 / *It's Not the End*

WHAT TO EXPECT

While getting fired is one of the most shattering experiences in life, it will at least occasionally turn out to be a break, leading to opportunities that otherwise would have been missed.

Take the case of Bert Parks, the television personality who was let out after many years as emcee of the Miss America Pageant. His reaction, he recalled, was "disbelief and shock." But he soon overcame his negative feelings, he said, because he was now free to explore different kinds of TV work and other opportunities "that had been denied me previously because of my association with the pageant."

"I have never felt more fulfilled professionally," Parks said. "I'd love to be fired again."

Or take the case of Sparky Anderson, one of the ablest managers in baseball. When fired by the Cincinnati Reds, he was "stunned and didn't really know what to say." But within a few days, he said, he realized he was actually in a position to become "a lot better off."

"I just made up my mind I was going to have a five-year contract with some special things in it that would really protect my wife in case of death," he said. "Also to be able to hire all my own coaches [and] to have a say in all trades."

Sure enough, Sparky soon had a new contract, with the Detroit Tigers.

Or consider the case of John D. Backe, who lost his job as president of CBS: "My experience since leaving CBS has been one of the most enlightening periods of my life," he said. "I have had the opportunity to evaluate situations that would radically change my career, opportunities that I did not know existed. At this point, I am not sure which turn my career will take, but I look forward to a new challenge with a renewed confidence that anything is possible and no challenge too great."

Of course, Bert Parks, Sparky Anderson and John Backe are hardly typical working people. Can a dismissal work out as well for someone with more conventional credentials and less visibility?

It did for John R. Lane of Harbor City, California, who lost his job as a police officer. He used words like "shock," "disbelief" and "devastated" to describe his first reaction. But those feelings eventually passed.

"I decided to go to school full-time and use my G.I. Bill," he said. "In retrospect, it was for the better."

Things also worked out for George Fusco, former assistant administrator of the Veterans Home and Hospital at Rocky Hill, Connecticut:

"When I first heard of my pending departure," Fusco said, "I was in complete shock. I was called into the administrative office and told I was to be replaced by another person who had no previous experience in hospital administration. My pulse quickened. I wanted to be alone. . . . I was stunned and angry at the same time.

"I had this position for five years and worked hard at my job. Being a disabled vet myself, I really believed in what I was doing. . . . I worked day and night to make this the best veterans' home and hospital in the United States. I had no vacations, nor did I stay out sick on any day in the five years I worked at the facility.

"I became very fond of all the veterans. They were a different breed from what you find in everyday life. This was the end of the line for them. Most would never leave until they expired. . . . They were the finest people that this country and state could assemble when our country was in danger. They went [out] to defend us in our greatest need, and now they are forgotten by most people."

Here, clearly, was a person with a real commitment to his job. A year and a half after he left, he said, he still felt anger because he was fired "for absolutely no reason." But:

"I now feel relieved and relaxed as never before in my life as I now realize that I gave too much of myself. I spend more time with my family and friends. . . .

"I am working as a project engineer for a large company and am enjoying it very much."

A friend of mine, Matt Franich, now a highly successful builder, told me he suffered "severe loss of self-esteem" when fired years ago. "But I was determined not to accept defeat and looked at this as an opportunity for independence and a chance to build my own future," he said. "I'm sorry it took as long as it did for me to discover the route to being self-employed. I should have made the transition ten years earlier. I went from being a $300-a-month engineer [in 1951] to millionaire status only after I left employment. In [the last] twelve years I have parlayed that status twelve times. Each year seems to get better and the opportunities appear greater and almost unlimited. All thanks to someone else making the decision for me. Never give up!"

The "someone else," of course, was the person who fired him.

When Bob Fontaine was relieved as general manager of the San Diego Padres, he was psychologically flattened. The firing came without warning, he said, and "twelve years of my life was now a memory."

Fontaine had offers from a number of teams within twenty-four hours, and eventually joined the San Francisco Giants as director of player personnel. He said the experience did more than teach him he could get another job.

"The good emotions are the fact it brings you closer to your family, and you really appreciate the luxury we own in our friends," he said. "There is a reawakening to fight and accept a new challenge and further your ambition to be a better man and performer. Despite your abilities, vacancies don't always develop the moment you need one. But with renewed vigor and a cleared head, you know that in the future another challenge of your choosing awaits."

Unlike Fontaine, former Boston Red Sox manager Don Zimmer was not altogether surprised when he was released.

"I was half expecting it because the club was going bad," Zimmer said. "After thirty-two years in pro baseball, it was hard being fired for the first time. . . . But it made me feel good when the job offers started coming in after just a short time."

Even before that, however, Zimmer had managed to develop a positive outlook.

"I had made up my mind the day I was fired that I would not sit out a year," he said. "I would be back in uniform somewhere. My first choice was a major league manager's job, which I got [with the Texas Rangers], but I would have settled for a coaching job or even gone back to the minor leagues."

Jack McKinney's state of mind was understandably less positive when he lost his job with the Los Angeles Lakers. On November 8, 1979, after only thirteen games as head coach in L.A., McKinney suffered severe head injuries in a fluke bicycle accident. His assistant, Paul Westhead, took over as acting head coach and the Lakers went on to win the National Basketball Association championship. McKinney was then fired by club owner Jerry Buss. Westhead replaced him.

"After the firing," *Sports Illustrated* reported, "McKinney behaved as if in a daze. He stopped working out. He sat in his house, not talking, feeling despondent, humiliated and hurt. . . .

" 'After I got axed, I simply wanted to quit life,' McKinney says. 'I plunged into a deep depression, and I didn't know what to do or where to turn. I was really confused. Claire and the kids were so great during that period, so understanding, but I just couldn't come out of it. I was just so stunned.'

"Finally, McKinney sought the advice of a psychiatrist. 'Yeah, I guess he helped,' says McKinney. 'He encouraged me not to give up. He said I was too young to abandon my career. He convinced me I still had a lot to offer.'

"McKinney was bothered most—and is still bothered—by the fact that he was fired before [a] promised meeting with Buss and Westhead took place. He understands that it probably wouldn't have altered anything. But it would . . . have lessened the hurt, preserved his dignity."

McKinney told *Sports Illustrated* the experience changed his view of people:

"I was once a very naive man. In the past I always believed everyone. Now, reluctantly, I am more careful around people. I'm also less outgoing. I've become more introverted. And I don't get as excited as I used to about things. Most of all, I'm cautious, very cautious in dealing with people."[1]

McKinney later became head coach of the Indiana Pacers and sounded more upbeat when he wrote to answer a questionnaire I circulated in preparation for this book. Two of the questions and answers:

Q.: How did you overcome the negative feelings?

MCKINNEY: By thinking positive. I know that is easier said than done. But I'm a very positive person. After getting over the hurt, I realize I was not the only guy in the world to lose a job. And that life must go on [and I should] stop feeling sorry for myself. So—think positive.

Q.: How do you feel about it now?

MCKINNEY: I feel, and hope I'm being honest, that it is behind me. It's in the past and I have no feeling. I would be stupid to think about the past when the present and the future hold so much.

McKinney was doubtless reminded of the past, however, in November of 1981, when Buss fired Westhead while the Lakers were on a five-game winning streak. It happened a day after the team's youngest superstar, Magic Johnson, announced he wanted to be traded, saying he and the coach didn't "see eye to eye on a lot of things." Buss said he had decided to dismiss Westhead before Johnson unloaded on the coach. But not everyone was persuaded. At least one reporter resurrected the line about the inmates having seized control of the asylum. And columnist Jim Murray wrote, "Now we know why they call him Magic. He made the boss disappear."[2]

McKinney reached a similar conclusion, saying it appeared the club was being run by the players. "It's ridiculous on the part of the Los Angeles organization," he said. "I'm upset with the situation out there. The guy [Westhead] won a championship for them."[3]

A LEARNING EXPERIENCE

Sparky Anderson, Don Zimmer, Jack McKinney and some of the others we've just heard from were lucky. They lost jobs but found something better, or at least about as good. To avoid being accused of trafficking in unwarranted optimism, I should add that not everyone will recover that nicely that easily. Further, getting fired hurts even if recovery is assured, and it may cause at least occasional pain long afterward. But many find the experience enlightening as well as painful. Take these observations from a guest column in *Newsweek:*

"Layoffs, unemployment and recession have always affected Walter Cronkite's tone of voice and the editorial pages. And maybe they affected a neighborhood business or a friend's uncle. But these terms have always been just words, something affecting someone else's world, like a passing ambulance. At least they were until a few weeks ago, when the ambulance came for me.

"Even as I sat staring blankly at my supervisor, hearing, 'I've got bad news: We're going to have to let you go,' it all still seemed no more applicable to my daily life than a '60 Minutes' exposé. I kept waiting for the alternative—'but you can come back after a couple of months,' or 'you could take a salary cut, a different position,' or even, 'April fool.' But none of these came. This was final. . . .

"We unemployed share a social stigma similar to that of the rape victim. Whether consciously or subconsciously, much of the work-ethic-driven public feels that you've somehow 'asked for it,' secretly wanted to lose your job and 'flirted' with unemployment through your attitude—probably dressed in a way to invite it (left the vest unbuttoned on your three-piece suit). . . .

"But you . . . maintain balance and perspective. . . . Although something going wrong in any aspect of your life now seems to push you into temporary despair much more easily than before, you have some very important things to hang on to— people who care, your sense of humor, your talents, your cat and your hopes.

"And beyond that, you've gained something—a little more knowledge and a lot more compassion. You've learned the value of the routine you scorned and the importance of the job you took for granted. But most of all, you've learned what a '7.6 percent unemployment rate' means."[4]

(The column carried a happy footnote: "Since she wrote this during four months of unemployment, Jan Halvorsen has become assistant editor of the *Twin Cities Courier* in St. Paul, Minnesota.")

Chuck Lane also profited from reflection after losing his front-office job with the Green Bay Packers. He wrote me:

"In formulating my plans to get back on track, I resolved not to let this temporary professional setback defeat me personally. I will judge myself, and others will judge me, on my ability to maintain my professionalism and how I maintain dignity and grace under fire. It won't be forever, and even though the hurt and frustration are still felt, I won't let the negative feelings of rejection and reaction consume me. They can fire me from a job, and they can hurt me, but they will never make me surrender ideals and beliefs that were developed with seventeen years of hard-earned experience in this field."

From a famous standup comic who was told to sit down after a long run on television, I received this:

"I hear you are writing a book titled *Merry Christmas—You're Fired!* How would you like to be fired on Passover? . . . NBC signed me to a thirty-year contract to perform and consult, and since Passover of 1960 I haven't performed on NBC, and they lost my telephone number."

Had the number been listed, it would have been under the name of Milton Berle, whose letter continued:

"When I was eight years old, I was fired for the ninth time in Vaudeville. I played towns with names like Fleabag, Missouri. Once I played a town so small the local hooker was a virgin and the head of the local Mafia was a Filipino."

Berle, who really has nothing against small Missouri towns or Filipinos (I'm not so sure about virgins), then grew uncharacteristically serious:

"If you're a perfectionist, if you persevere and have discipline and dedication, if you know who you are and what you stand for and that most of the time you're doing things right—and have that certain confidence in yourself and your actions—then talent will always out. . . .

"When those adverse moments crop up, and you know the outcome was not your fault, just remember that in your own mind you know you were trying to do the best job possible. You gave it your best shot. . . . So have the courage of your convictions and don't devalue yourself."

Jack Kent Cooke, chairman of the board of the Washington Redskins, also wrote. I knew Jack hadn't lost his job (there being no one in the organization in a position to fire him), but I thought he might have some sound advice on how to deal with setbacks.

"Frankly, George, I have never considered any setback I have had for much longer than twenty-four hours," he wrote. "Always I have looked to the rest of the day and tomorrow, firmly resolved that I will overcome whatever setback I have suffered. Dwelling on a misfortune is the surest waste of energy I can think of; the only possible benefit in reviewing a setback is how best to avoid recommitting the source of the setback."

Still, as football coach Frank Kush discovered, it's hard not to think back, even though it hurts. Two years after he lost his head coaching job at Arizona State, Kush was still in pain. He had by then moved on to the Canadian Football League, as head coach at Hamilton, and was soon to enter the next phase of his comeback by joining the Baltimore Colts in the same capacity. But a *Washington Post* story made it clear Kush hadn't forgotten what happened at Arizona State:

"Kush is not a big man," the story said, "but his body is rock-solid, still in superb condition. His face has the rough-hewn lines of a working man, a miner, which he would have been if not for football. But what you notice most are the deep-set eyes. When Frank Kush talks about Arizona State, they flash. His whole face seems to tighten around them. The lines appear deeper, the slack jaw tightens.

" 'I'm not bitter,' he said. . . . 'If you have feelings of bitterness, sorrow or anger, they're all in you and you're the one who suffers. [But] after twenty-five years they took me and threw me out like an old washrag. That hurts. I know I still have scars from it. I don't have any pictures of those years because right now I just couldn't look at them. Maybe when I'm old and decrepit, I'll take them out and be able to look. All that is history; it's gone. I don't want to linger. I don't need that now.' "[5]

Kush was one of fifteen children of a Pennsylvania miner who died when Frank was still a boy. As a teenager, Kush worked on the railroad. He probably would have wound up in the mines, too, if he and football hadn't discovered each other. He went to Arizona State as an assistant to Dan Devine in 1955 and became head coach when Devine moved on to Missouri in 1958. Kush was then only twenty-nine.

"By the early 1970s," the *Post* story said, "he was an Arizona legend. He turned down a number of lucrative offers to leave; he was reportedly making close to $200,000 a year. In 1974, ASU went 12-0, finishing the season with a Fiesta Bowl upset of Nebraska that earned them the No. 2 ranking in the country. Kush was chosen coach of the year. . . .

"But in September 1979, it began to fall apart. [Kevin] Rutledge, the team's punter, went to the ASU board of regents and said that Kush had struck him after a poor punt during the 1978

Washington game. The regents rejected Rutledge's allegation, but his family filed suit against Kush. . . . Then three players . . . said they had seen Kush hit Rutledge. . . . On October 13, 1979, before the school could announce his firing, Kush announced it.''

A jury found against Rutledge, but his father said a new trial would be sought and an appeal taken if necessary. As this is written, the case is still not over.

Many football coaches probably followed the trial anxiously. A verdict for Rutledge could have had the effect of limiting their disciplinary authority. The *Post* quoted supportive statements by two fellow coaches, Jerry Claiborne of Maryland (who later moved to the University of Kentucky) and John Robinson of Southern California.

"Frank Kush is a good man and a good coach," Claiborne said. "When kids went to play for him they knew what they were getting; they knew what kind of personality he had. He had coached that way for years."

"It wasn't like a Jekyll-and-Hyde thing," Robinson said. "That's always the way Frank has been. I think Frank was a victim of crossing generations. For a long time his methods were expected; most people used them. Times changed. Frank got caught in the change."

Kush told the *Post* he had not struck the player, "to the best of my knowledge."

"The answer, like the incident, is blurred," the story said. "It always will be. It will always haunt Frank Kush. But, he says, it won't break him.

" 'I've been asked by people a lot of times, "Is this the highlight of your career?" When we went to a bowl they asked; when we beat Nebraska they asked; when I was coach of the year they asked. Every time I've given the same answer: "Like hell it is." Something else will always come up that's just as enjoyable or better. When I left ASU people said this was the end. I said the same thing. "Like hell it is." ' "

That's exactly the sort of mental toughness you need in such a situation. You shouldn't just think you're going to lick the problem. You should know it.

Kenneth Kirkpatrick said he knew it. He kept itching to get his job back after being fired, and it turned out to be a case of the seven-year itch. A news story summarized his long ordeal:

"After a seven-year battle to regain his job, Kenneth Kirkpatrick yesterday finally was ordered reinstated as chief probation officer of Los Angeles County, a post he lost for alleged incompetence.

"He also will receive $273,000 in back pay and fringe benefits.

"The sixty-six-year-old Kirkpatrick's hopes of winning back his probation job were raised and dashed many times in the past, as hearing followed hearing and appeal followed appeal. . . . But each time a court ruled he was fired unjustly and should go back to work, the County Board of Supervisors found a way to prolong the legal process. . . .

"This time, however, Kirkpatrick's victory was real. When Superior Court Judge David A. Thomas delivered his ruling yesterday, spectators cheered and applauded for the career civil servant. . . .

"Kirkpatrick is the only county department head ever terminated on grounds of incompetence. . . . [He] said he never doubted that eventually he would again run the 3,600-employee Probation Department and has no plans to retire despite his age. 'It was a matter of principle with me,' he said. 'They tried to get rid of the wrong guy. If I had been wrong, I would have been the first to admit it. But when I'm right I fight for it.' "[6]

It wasn't easy for him financially, and it was probably even harder emotionally. His wife died along the way.

Kirkpatrick was accused of mismanaging his department. But Judge Thomas found he was guilty of only two of fourteen alleged transgressions and said they "were of small moment."[7]

Radio personality Larry King also made it back after a long pull. In fact, he made it back and then some, becoming host of a nighttime talk show heard on nearly two hundred and fifty stations. For a while there, though, he may have been about the only one who didn't think he was through.

King arrived in Miami from Brooklyn in 1957. In his pocket he had $13. In his head he had the idea of becoming a broadcaster.

He hooked on as a disc jockey at a small station. Then, in 1960, the owner of a well-known delicatessen in Miami Beach got the idea of having a radio talk show originate from the deli. As host of that show, King became an overnight star. And he began spending money. Too much.

"I decided it was stupid to lease a Ford when I could lease a Cadillac," he told an interviewer years later. "I was caught up in a whirl and for ten years I was both Peter and Paul, rich and poor. I had high visibility and I knew I had a lot of talent. I began to feel that nothing bad could happen to me."

But it did. He began playing the horses, and they began running off with his money. "I was living way over my head," he said, "and gambling was only part of it." The writer who interviewed him told some of the rest of it:

"The inevitable crash began in 1971. Financier Louis Wolfson gave King $5,000 to pass on to Jim Garrison, the New Orleans district attorney investigating the Kennedy assassination. Wolfson claimed King pocketed the money instead and had him . . . charged with grand larceny. . . . The charge was later dismissed because the statute of limitations ran out. [But] his radio program, TV show, newspaper column and marriage all ended with a crash. He was more than $300,000 in debt."[8]

King bounced around several years, doing seasonal public relations work and other small jobs. But he was still thinking about making it big again in broadcasting.

Damned if he didn't. In 1975, he got a call from the Miami radio station that had carried his show. The station had a new general manager. He wondered if King would like to rejoin the station. Not long afterward King made his return. He recalled the first night:

"The engineer plays the 'Larry King Show' theme and says, 'Here's Larry!' And I said, 'As I was saying . . .' And it was all back again."

The show took off almost immediately and a few years later King started doing his network talk show for the Mutual Broadcasting System.

"I never did think I wouldn't go back," he said.

For coaches and professional athletes, like broadcasters and others in the public eye, getting fired is doubly embarrassing. Not only have you lost a job, but the whole world seems to know about it. When a salesman is "cut" by his insurance company, it may make for some talk around the office. But when a football player is cut, or a coach fired, it makes the newspapers. And that makes it harder to deal with. But some people manage. For example:

"Jim Krahl, a defensive tackle signed by the 49ers after the third game and cut two weeks later, is trying to establish business contacts. Punter Eddie Hare, dropped from the injured-reserve list by the Patriots after his second game, is doing the same, though he'll get a tryout from the Browns next week. . . .

" 'I've always enjoyed football, but I've never let it rule my life,' said Hare. . . . 'A lot of guys build their whole life around football and when that's gone, that's all there is.'

"Krahl, who has played with three teams in three seasons, has had just about enough.

" 'If I get a chance [to play again] and nothing else turns up, I'll probably go with it,' he said. 'But if I get a job with a future and security, I wouldn't get back into it.' "[9]

Jim Tyrer, an offensive tackle who played for me briefly at Washington after making All-Pro with the Kansas City Chiefs, was tragically unable to cope with the problem.

Tyrer wasn't fired. But it was about the same thing. He was forced into retirement by age in 1975. In 1980, he killed his wife, then committed suicide.

I came across this explanation by Tyrer's minister in a Washington newspaper:

"Few if any of us have had to make such a transition. He had been at the top, from junior high school through high school through college and through the NFL. He had been idolized. . . .

"But it got to the point where Jim considered himself a failure. Whether that's right or not isn't important, because he believed it and couldn't deal with reality."[10]

Dave Hill, a former teammate of Tyrer's, also was quoted in the article:

"I can't remember the last time I saw Jim. But he was on the phone about three weeks ago, looking for a job, wondering if I knew anyone who needed a good man. . . . Not much went right for him in business. At thirty-seven [or] thirty-eight, he was just starting over at a time men he went to college with were in their prime earning years."

Another writer used the 1981 presidential transition as the peg for a story illustrating the special torment felt by high-visibility people who lose their jobs:

"There is no legion of secretaries to answer the phone for Bob Bergland any more. . . . The chauffeur-driven limousine no longer waits at the door, and acquaintances are not as deferential as in the old days.

"All in all, it has been quite a comedown for Bergland since he lost his $69,630 job as secretary of agriculture in the Jimmy Carter administration on January 20 and had to start pounding the streets looking for work.

" 'There's this idea that anyone who's been a cabinet officer won't have any trouble, that people will offer you a big job,' Bergland said. 'Well, they haven't.' "[11]

As it turned out, Bergland soon landed a job with an export firm. But not before he had experienced that feeling of sudden nakedness that comes over those stripped of power and turned into the streets.

The same news story offered these comments from people who had suffered through the experience and/or observed the suffering:

Barry Jagoda, a White House aide under President Carter—"Anyone who doesn't admit to a good deal of depression and regret on leaving political office isn't telling the truth. It is an enormous change from holding enormous power to holding no power."

Washington psychiatrist Harvey Rich—"There's a big problem for these people in having to become the seeker rather than the sought."

Norman Sherman, press secretary to former Vice President

Hubert H. Humphrey—"My most graphic memory of losing office is that I received eighteen bottles of liquor from unions and other well-wishers at Christmas in 1967. [A year later] I received no bottles of liquor—zero."

Bergland—"To be defeated is a tough thing. Some congressmen are just flabbergasted to lose. They take it as a personal affront. . . . It was a lot easier for me [as an appointed official] to take the loss last November than it was for President Carter. He did take it as a personal rejection."

Moon Landrieu, secretary of housing and urban development under Carter, had perhaps the healthiest observation:

"I've never confused myself with any office I've held. None of us were born to royalty or political office. The voters give— and the voters take away."

MENTAL CONDITIONING

Happily, most job losses do not bring on full-blown tragedies. But the realization that losing a job is apt to be only a short-term setback is often perceived only dimly, if at all, in the early stages of adjustment. It's hard to get much positive thinking done when you're in shock. Dismissal is usually not like a tide that rises slowly, gradually wetting your pants cuffs. It's a tidal wave that bowls you over, submerging you in despair. You'll probably surface shortly. The trouble is you don't realize it at the time. It's something like going through a divorce. Most people can get over it eventually, but they don't know that when the torment is greatest.

In the last chapter, I discussed practical steps to put the family economy on as sound a footing as the emergency will allow. Now it's time to go to work on your mental outlook, to repair some of the damage caused when you were flattened by that tidal wave.

I can count at least four noneconomic problems you'll probably have to come to grips with: (1) separation from friends and associates, (2) loss of purpose and identity, (3) feelings of guilt, fear, bitterness, confusion and self-pity and (4) too much time on your hands.

In some cases, you'll discover to your dismay that people you thought were your friends have deserted you. There is no way to prepare for this disappointment, but you can learn to live with it rather easily, because losing friends like these is really no loss at all.

The worst part of being let down by supposed friends is that it makes you suspicious of people, adding to your accumulation of negative feelings.

Luckily, some of your friends will stand by you, and their support will count a lot. But you probably won't see as much of them as you did before. Friends you worked with will still be on the job eight hours a day, and you're no longer part of the scene at the plant or office. You're an outsider now.

You can't call them at work just to talk, for the same reason you wouldn't want people calling you at work just to talk. You can't expect them to spend company time on your problems.

Nor should you expect them to devote most of their free time to your problems. They're your friends, but they have problems of their own. At bottom, about all they can give you is regular reassurance, and maybe an occasional job tip. They can make life more livable in that hole you're in, but they can't climb out of it for you.

The next problem is loss of purpose. "When men are employed," Benjamin Franklin said, "they are best contented. For on the days they worked they were good-natured and cheerful, and, with the consciousness of having done a good day's work, they spent the evening jollily." But on idle days, he said, "they were mutinous and quarrelsome."

In our society, people are often identified with their work. When they lose their jobs, they often lose their identity, and much of their purpose. The difference between who we *are* and who we *were* can make for an enormous difference in outlook. The coauthors of a book on aging made the point nicely:

"Because the later years provide no exciting new roles to replace the occupational roles lost on retirement, the retiree cannot proudly say, 'I am a . . .' Instead, he must say, 'I *was* a good doctor,' or, 'I *was* a successful businessman.' Only by looking back can the retiree find a self-image he or she can be proud of. No wonder the elderly enjoy reminiscing.''[12]

Often people who have been fired can't even enjoy reminiscing, because it reminds them of the job they just lost, and confronts them with the third of the four problems I described: trying to deal with feelings of guilt, fear, bitterness, confusion and self-pity.

In preparing this book, I dictated a twenty-five-page segment on how it felt to be fired. I found that even though I was supposedly "adjusted" to my last firing in 1978, it was painful to go back and reopen the wounds. Excerpts from that segment reveal the range of emotions the memory evoked:

> When Carroll [Rosenbloom] fired me, I couldn't believe it. I couldn't believe what was happening.
> I was hurt, deeply disappointed, because I came to L.A. to lead the Rams to the Super Bowl. Then to be fired after only *two* preseason games! Having coached twenty-nine years, and then to lose my job that way . . .
> What did I do wrong? Where did I fail? I still don't know. I didn't let down anywhere. I didn't fail anywhere. I didn't do anything wrong. I did exactly what I'd done in all my years in coaching: worked hard, tried to motivate people, and used the same program that I'd always used.
> At times I thought I might be going crazy when I'd start thinking about it. I got so depressed. I'd think, Am I ever going to come out of this? Am I ever going to coach again?
> A lot of people I counted on didn't come through for me. A lot of people I thought were my friends let me down . . .
> Your daughter cries. Your son cries. Your wife cries. The next day the moving van comes [with furniture sent out from Washington] and you're unpacking—for what? Are you going to live here, or three thousand miles back across the country?
> The first night after you're fired, you don't sleep at all. Or the second night. Or the third. In fact, even now, when I think back on what happened, every once in a while I have trouble sleeping. It seems like you're always exhausted after a firing, because you can't get enough rest.

I didn't eat much, and I lost a lot of weight. I was impatient, and lost my temper over the slightest thing. I embarrassed myself at a restaurant once when I ordered fish, and then bawled out the waiter when he told me they didn't have it. I took things personally when I never had before.

It's not that you decide to become a new, less pleasant person. It's just that the pressure is so immense, and coming at you from every side. You're unable to make decisions or deal rationally with people or problems. The more frustrated you become, the more you tend to take out your hostilities on the people you care about the most, because they're the only people who want to be around you.

Most people work out these problems sooner or later, but not without considerable pain. With no job to keep you occupied, you're particularly vulnerable to painful thoughts. You're under the spell of the last of the four curses I was talking about: You've got all that time on your hands.

One of the dilemmas you face after being fired is that you both need to be alone and need not to be. You need some solo time to straighten out your thinking and come to terms with your predicament, but you don't need time to brood about it. The trick is to balance the two needs properly.

The best approach is to try to stay busy. And on those inevitable occasions when you're reminded of your job loss and tempted to brood, you should tell yourself—order yourself—to think about something else. Visualize yourself switching your mind to a different channel. It may take some effort at first to twist the knob. In the early going you'll have some bad spells no matter what you do. But keep fighting it.

Strangely, with all that time at your disposal, you may be tempted to do less work in an entire day than you'd normally do outside work hours. In the past you may have been concerned about your personal appearance. Now there's a tendency to let yourself go, by not shaving, by dressing sloppily, gaining weight, not grooming your hair.

I got into this kind of rut. I'd skip shaving. I have a tough beard and often shave twice a day. But I'd find myself skipping a day, and then the next day. I had always asked my players to be neat and clean-shaven. I stressed the point, along with many others, at team meetings, and even put it in our playbooks. Now the teacher was disregarding his own lesson.

This lasted about ten days. I was doing a television show in Los Angeles and couldn't go on looking like a derelict. It occurred to me while I was dressing and shaving how much I'd let myself go. That realization shook me out of it. But I can see how a person who doesn't have to get out could ignore his personal appearance indefinitely after losing a job. Why should he look his best for a world that has turned against him?

I can think of at least two reasons. First, you're looking for a job, and, when you line up some job interviews, people will be looking at you. There's not much danger, I suppose, that an out-of-work salesman would turn up for a job interview unshaven. But suppose he has let himself get really overweight. If he has an interview tomorrow, he can't lose thirty-five pounds overnight. If you don't concern yourself with your appearance, you may be putting more time between you and your next job.

Good personal appearance is also a mark of self-discipline. And self-discipline improves self-image, which inspires confidence, which makes you more effective in job interviews. Self-discipline is vital to recovery when you're unemployed.

WHAT TO DO

I've discussed four problems that can impair your attitude when you lose a job. Now I'll list five steps you can take to get your head together.

—Surround yourself with positive things.
—Attack your problems one at a time.
—Discipline yourself to become a self-starter.

—Organize the details of your life.

—And, as I've always told my players, try to think professionally, meaning maturely.

Following these five steps is not just a means of adjusting. It's a good way of life. Let's take them one at a time.

Surround Yourself With Positive Things. Selwyn Slerdspeech played golf every week, though if you'd seen his scorecard you might have thought he'd been bowling. Whenever he hit a lousy shot, which was usually whenever he brought his club into play, he would reach for a bottle in his bag and take a drink. By the sixth hole, he had rid himself entirely of negative thoughts about his golf game. Selwyn presented no hazard to others on the course because he played every round by himself, out of bounds. And he exposed himself to no painful recollections of wretched shots because he could never remember what happened. Selwyn had gotten the better of the game—and may have been the only golfer in history to do so. Alas, Selwyn died at sixty-three (his usual nine-hole score) when struck by a truck while addressing his ball for an approach shot off the No. 3 lane of a freeway adjacent to his country club.

Trying to escape negative thoughts after a job loss by drinking may not get you killed. But it won't get you work, either. I'd recommend a more sober approach to positive thinking.

As will be described in more detail later, I organized an office downstairs in my home after my last firing. I put pictures of my family on my desk, filled bookshelves with trophies I'd won and hung plaques on the walls. I wanted to surround myself with positive memories. Everything I could find that I was really proud of was right there in front of me while I worked at my desk. I don't care much about jewelry, but I started wearing my National Football Conference championship ring (from Washington) and my National Football League championship ring (from my days as an assistant coach with the Chicago Bears). I had received more than a dozen keys to cities across the country, and I had them put in acrylic bases. I used them as paperweights and decorative pieces. I compiled scrapbooks of newspaper and magazine articles about me and members of the family.

All of us have accomplished things we're really proud of. The things that trigger positive responses in your mind may not be the same ones that work for me. But you might try putting your favorite mementos out where you can see them, as a constant reminder of what you have been, and can be again.

If you're used to working in an office, and don't have one at home, I suggest you set aside an area where you can do a little work or just be by yourself for a while. It can give you the feeling of having a headquarters.

Don't go to depressing movies or watch depressing shows on television. Don't read depressing books. You can benefit greatly from reading inspirational books, particularly those in which people surmount major obstacles. (If you're looking for a suggestion, see if your library has a copy of a book called *Endurance*.[13] It's the story of how Sir Ernest Shackleton, the great south polar explorer, brought his crew back to civilization in whaleboats after their ship was crushed by ice along the coast of Antarctica in the early 1900s. It's an account of a leader whose prodigious courage saved a party that probably would have perished almost overnight without him. The book could be out of print by now, but if you've got a little of Shackleton's perseverance you may be able to find a copy. It's really a remarkable story.)

As I suggested earlier, one of the most positive things you can surround yourself with is your family. Mine has always been a positive force in my life. But the demands of coaching were such that I had never been able to spend enough time with my wife and kids, until my last firing. It was a new experience for me to have dinner with them regularly, to take them to movies, plays and ballgames. They were a great reservoir of support.

Attack Your Problems One at a Time. Let's say you're trying to put together a jigsaw puzzle. You decide to speed things up by working with twenty pieces at once. You'll never get the picture that way. A jigsaw puzzle is put together one piece at a time. There's no other way to do it. Most problems are solved the same way.

When you've lost a job, you're confused and easily distracted. With so many problems pressing down on you, it's hard to keep concentrating on one thing. So you take on one problem, get sidetracked by another a few minutes later, then leave that one undone when a third problem pops up. It won't work. My approach was to try to fasten my attention on *one* problem each day. When unavoidably distracted by another problem, I would give it my complete attention and resolve it before returning to the original task for the day. Perhaps a better way of saying it is that I tried to concentrate on what I was doing while I was doing it, to the exclusion of everything else.

It was relatively easy for me, because my coaching experience had taught me the knack of dealing with constant interruptions in an organized manner. In pro football, if you aren't careful, a practice session can become a series of interruptions with drills squeezed in between.

Take time every night to write out a schedule for the following day. A diary or journal is ideal for this purpose. List all your planned activities, but don't plan three dozen of them. The schedule is no good if it can't be followed. Include one problem to be solved, or at least worked on, each day. Simplifying your routine will help you stay organized.

Discipline Yourself to Become a Self-starter. In coaching, I always looked for players who were self-starters—motivated from within. I never had to ask them to give an extra effort. They gave 110 percent on every play, not because I thought it was important, but because they thought so.

Most self-starters probably couldn't tell you exactly why they are motivated to achieve at high levels. Some may identify with dynamic personalities from their past. Others may be motivated by a desire to be recognized or to overcome a disadvantaged childhood. Whatever moves them, self-starters tend to make excellent workers. They have goals and they make things happen to bring the goals closer.

Anyone can become a self-starter. Even if you've never considered yourself organized or disciplined, all you have to do is avail yourself of an ingredient known to all but used by few: hard work.

Hard work is easy, once you get the hang of it. It's easier than the other kind because it makes the workday go faster. And it gives you a better image of yourself. You've accomplished more. If you approach a job indifferently, you'll only drag it out, making it more laborious. That comes pretty close to defining drudgery.

It is important to understand that discipline and motivation are mental attributes, not physical characteristics. The self-starting football player can give 110 percent on every play because he has already performed the equally demanding task of preparing himself mentally.

The "hard work" facing an unemployed person is more than simply typing up job inquiries and making telephone calls. These are only physical aspects of dealing with the problem. The important preliminary step is to come to an understanding with yourself—to resolve that you will *not* be beaten, that you're going to make things happen, that you're going to bring a sense of purpose and commitment to everything you do.

Organize the Details of Your Life. One of the first things I did after moving back into our house on the Palos Verdes Peninsula was to organize a work space downstairs. Since I was going to spend a lot of time in it, I wanted to make it a place where I would enjoy working and relaxing. I had a telephone installed. I brought a stereo down, put up a wall clock, even installed a water cooler. I cleaned out a clothes closet and used it for storing office supplies.

I think it's important to set aside space for an office at home if, like me, you're accustomed to an office environment. Unemployment makes you feel rootless. Working in an office at home restores a sense of routine to your life. As I said earlier, it gives you a headquarters.

Another of the changes I made at home was to set up a kind of mini-gym in the garage. I called it the George Allen Health Club. I put in a Universal weight machine, punching bag, heavy bag, chin-up bar, stall bar for leg exercises and a rowing machine. And I used them.

Etty and I planted a garden behind the house. We put in citrus trees, berry plants and grapes. I've always enjoyed gardening, but I'd never been able to get myself away from coaching long enough to get seriously into it.

Working in a garden helped occupy my time. It also gave me a feeling of accomplishment and order. I took a great deal of pride in it.

I believe that everything in life has a purpose. And our lives themselves have a purpose. Organizing the details of our lives brings that purpose into sharper focus. The sharper it is, the less likely we will lose sight of it after a severe setback. Whether the task is as important as lining up job contacts or as seemingly unimportant as organizing a home office, attention to detail will prove invaluable. No general would send his troops into battle without a plan. Yet we are often guilty of doing essentially the same thing by facing life without a real plan.

Planning even pays off when applied to nonserious pursuits. In San Diego some years ago, there was a club with an amusing motto: "We ain't got no goals, so we can't hardly miss." In fact, the membership included many hard-working and successful people. The periodic club meetings, at which nothing of importance could be discussed, were merely enjoyable diversions. Their motto notwithstanding, the club members indeed had a purpose. It was not just to break up the day by having lunch together, but also by having a few laughs together. The point is that they really did have a goal—wholesome relaxation—and they pursued it with a will. Those luncheon meetings didn't just happen; they were planned by imaginative people who, I suspect, made a regular habit of planning the details of their lives.

Organization is a habit. It's such a useful and important habit that it's surprising more people haven't acquired it. All that's necessary to establish an orderly pattern in your life is to make a habit of planning how you'll spend your time. This ties in with my earlier suggestion that you plan a daily schedule, targeting one problem to attack each day. But plan the whole day, including nonproblem activities. Even if the activities that come to mind seem trivial, write them down. The important thing is not whether the activities themselves are important, but whether you've got a plan for tomorrow or are content merely to drift through the day aimlessly. A schedule tells you that you've got things to do. It pushes you. We all need pushing.

When I was coaching in Washington, the Redskins agreed, at my request, to furnish me with a car and driver. Some people suggested I was looking for more than an easy way to get around; they thought the car was for taking me on ego trips.

But I had found that one of the keys to success in coaching was full utilization of time. There is always more time available to do a job than appears, if you manage your time properly. I wanted a driver so I could get some work done while on the road. I might just sit in the back seat concentrating, planning for the next team meeting, practice or game. Sometimes I would have an assistant along and we would have a meeting right there in the back seat. Sometimes my secretary would join me and we would get some mail answered. Occasionally I would even have back-seat meetings with my trainer or equipment man. It's really an ideal setting for a conference. With a driver, I didn't have to worry about traffic or how to get where I was going. There were no distractions. I got a lot of work done. And the arrangement had something more to recommend it: If I wasn't driving, the roads would be safer for everyone.

Another good time to work is while flying. I'll often bring along some work to do on a plane. In fact, my notes for the passage you're reading right now were written while I was flying from Los Angeles to Tampa, via Houston, to do color commentary for CBS at a game between the Tampa Bay Buccaneers and Detroit Lions. It was a 4 p.m. game, and I was going to get there with time to spare, so I also brought along my running gear and got in a little jogging before going to work.

My experience at running football teams inspired a little saying that I used for my own guidance: "Tell me how a person uses his time and I'll tell you whether I want to hire him." The next potential employer you contact may have the same philosophy.

To keep track of whether I'm spending my time properly, I carry my daily schedule around with me. As I get things done, I cross them off the schedule—or, if they're only one-half or one-fourth finished, I'll write a little ½ or ¼ beside them and carry them over to the next day. This is the best way I've found to budget time.

For me, it doesn't feel right to go to bed at night without completing or at least making some progress on one or more projects. If you can't point to any accomplishments, the day has been wasted. You can't store it in the freezer and use it again tomorrow. They don't make reusable days.

Think Maturely. Reason, not emotion, should rule your life. I've already mentioned some of the emotional states brought on by unemployment. But one thing I haven't discussed is dreaming.

Like Dr. Martin Luther King, each of us should have a dream. The absence of dreams (or goals) is one reason why many people are not committed to their work. But having a dream is quite different from living in a perpetual state of just hoping. That's having a pipe dream.

By dream I mean a realistic goal. A successful appliance salesman, for example, may realistically dream of opening his own appliance shop. If, instead, he sees himself being invited one day soon to give up selling vacuum cleaners to take over the presidency of General Electric, he's on the pipe.

I never got quite that carried away, but I did get my hopes up too high for a coaching job with the New York Giants one time. I felt that I was a natural for the job and could make the Giants a winner immediately. I just knew we could make the playoffs. I thought I had a real shot at the job because some good people were supporting me. But it didn't pan out. At that stage of my career, it was probably somewhat unrealistic of me to think it could. Anyway, the experience was a terrible emotional drain.

It's difficult to keep a tight rein on your emotions. But you have to try. Time is wasted if spent getting over needless disappointments.

The thing to do is to condition yourself to think maturely. Conditioning refers to habits. Making a habit of studying a situation carefully before reaching a conclusion is thinking maturely. Acting on impulse is not. If you're considering a move into a new line of work, and you make a point of reconnoitering the territory by questioning a number of people already doing that kind of work, you're thinking maturely. If you decide to become a lawyer because your mother said she would love to see you in a three-piece suit, you're not.

Serious thought, and maybe some professional job counseling if you can afford it, will tell you what's best for you. The next step is to condition yourself—force yourself—to *do* what is best. Take time to decide what you want out of life. Then develop a realistic plan for making life give it to you.

We're about to take up a game plan for the disemployed. But first I'd like to run through two case studies that make for a logical followup on the theme of this chapter: "It's not the end." The studies illustrate the truth of the theme by showing that there really is life after disemployment and that it can even be a better life.

1. Richard O'Connor, "After the Fall," *Sports Illustrated,* October 20, 1980.

2. Jim Murray, "Whatever Magic Wants, He Gets," *Los Angeles Times,* November 24, 1981.

3. "McKinney: 'Ridiculous on Part' of Lakers," *Los Angeles Times,* November 20, 1981.

4. Jan Halvorsen, "How It Feels to Be Out of Work," My Turn, *Newsweek,* September 22, 1980.

5. John Feinstein, "Frank Kush in Exile: Days of Future Past," *Washington Post,* October 4, 1981.

6. Richard Turner and Robert Knowles, "Gets Job Back and $273,000: Former Probation Chief Kirkpatrick Reinstated," *Los Angeles Herald Examiner,* October 1, 1981.

7. Myrna Oliver, "Probation Chief, Fired in '74, to Get Job Back Oct. 13," *Los Angeles Times,* October 1, 1981.

8. Alex Ben Block, "King of Late-Night Airwaves," *Los Angeles Herald Examiner,* November 3, 1981.

9. Bob Cohn, "Being Cut in the NFL Just Beginning of End," *Washington Post*, November 5, 1980.

10. Ken Denlinger, "Tyrer Tragedy: No Coping With Mortality," This Morning, *Washington Post*, September 21, 1980.

11. Bryce Nelson, "Out of a Job: Transition's Bitter Pill," *Los Angeles Times*, April 12, 1981.

12. Gordon and Walter Moss, with Gerald Leinwand, general editor, *Growing Old* (New York: Pocket Books, 1975).

13. Alfred Lansing, *Endurance: Shackleton's Incredible Voyage* (New York: McGraw-Hill, 1959).

4 / *December 26 Revisited*

"YOU HAVE BEEN REPLACED"

Wednesday, December 26, 1979. It was eleven years to the day after the Rams fired me for the first time, and it would become an unforgettable date for George F. Stocks, who now enters our story.

For most of his adult life, George had worked for a company we'll call Ubiquitous Auto Parts. (The real name is omitted because the company's treatment of Stocks may have been atypical and not instigated by top management.)

George, a local division manager, sat in his supervisor's office. He can still hear the supervisor saying, "You have been replaced. Your health is not good and you haven't gotten good results."

"It was the last thing I expected," George said. "I just sat there, stunned."

George was fifty-five years old. Except for one comparatively brief period, he had been part of his company since his early twenties. What was happening to him now could have destroyed

73

the spirit of a man half his age. It was as if he had just been disowned by his family.

But, as we shall see, that was not the end for George F. Stocks. He would be back.

It had been a long and laborious climb to the division managership. George had come from a poor Tennessee farm family and had grown up during the Great Depression.

"I'd guess 80 percent of the kids would bring their lunch to school or have lunch money," he said. "The other 20 percent of us went out on the playground and played during lunch hour. Sometimes I'd see kids who had food left over and were going to throw it away. I'd ask them to give it to me. I was hungry. I guess if you're hungry you forget your pride.

"I always wore clean clothes to school. But oftentimes they were worn, and sometimes torn. That hurt just a little because I did have a certain amount of pride."

That probably explains why George today is quite fastidious about his clothes. It's his defense against a recurrence of the embarrassment he felt as a schoolboy.

"It was a rough childhood," he said. "As a matter of fact I didn't really have a childhood. There were three kids in the family. We lived on a farm near Millington, and as soon as we got home from school we would get something to eat—maybe a biscuit and a slice of bacon—and then work until dark. We'd feed the livestock and milk the cows and then come in and have dinner. By then it was so late I wasn't able to get my studying done. I made good grades in the classroom but failed on homework because I couldn't get to it. I flunked the sixth grade."

George went to work for Ubiquitous Auto Parts in Tennessee in 1947. "I started with the company in a machine shop," he said. "We rebuilt engines, did valve jobs, repaired transmissions, turned brake drums. But I wanted to be more than a machinist. So in my spare time I would watch what the manager and the men on the parts counter were doing. I wanted to be a parts man because I thought you had to do that before you could become a manager. It turned out that wasn't true. They asked me to take over a new store, and I accepted. I was in management with the company until I went to the West Coast in 1960."

George had a daughter in poor health and made the move hoping it would help her. He got a job with a smaller parts company. It meant taking a step backward. He was a parts counterman again, for five years. He didn't like it. He wanted to get back in management, but for some reason—he never found out why—one of his superiors was holding him back. Then, in 1965, Ubiquitous bought out the smaller company and George was back with his old outfit. Within sixty days he was given a management position and the supervisor who had been holding him back was gone.

George managed a branch store in a Los Angeles suburb. In 1968 he was promoted to assistant local division manager and put in charge of operations at eight stores in the Los Angeles area.

In 1970 he took on a dual role, retaining his position as assistant local division manager and also running a suburban store. It was one of the largest stores in the Ubiquitous chain, and it was in trouble. George said that's why he was asked to take it over.

He got that problem straightened out, he said, and went back to being an assistant local division manager full-time.

But the man who had taken over the big suburban store ran it "right down the tube," he said. George had to go back and straighten it out again. That took until 1976. By this time, he said, he had made something of a name as a company troubleshooter.

"In December 1976," he said, "I was asked to come into the office. Two supervisors told me there was going to be a change. Before the day was out I was offered the position of local division manager of one of our Southern California units."

In 1977, he said, his unit showed a profit of 2.59 percent of net sales. The figure rose to 4.74 percent in 1978, and to 6.50 percent in 1979. The company expected 10 percent, he said, and he was gaining on it.

Then, in late November of 1979, he began feeling chest pains.

"I'd had high blood pressure for fourteen years," he said. "They found no other medical problem, but the doctor said I was exhausted because I was pushing too hard. He said he wanted me to stay off work until December 26.

"A week before I was to come back my supervisor called me. He seemed in a friendly mood. He asked if I was coming in on the twenty-sixth and when I told him yes, he said, 'Stop by my office.'

"I did."

And you know what happens to people who talk to their bosses on December 26.

"I was calm," George said. "At least I didn't throw anything at him. When he said I had not made progress I thought he was pretty far off base. When you can increase profit by 2 percent a year, I feel that's progress. I was stunned. At first I didn't say anything. And I can't really remember what I said when I did speak. But I remember the supervisor saying, 'We'll put you on a desk job here. It's an area where we're having a lot of problems, and we know you're capable of straightening them out.'

"But he wanted me to do it at one-half the money I'd been making."

So George had lost his job without actually being fired. The boss just wanted to kick him downstairs. Or was there more to it? Sometimes, instead of firing people outright, the boss will reassign them to positions he knows they will find intolerable. Then they'll quit. The boss will have achieved his real purpose without getting blood on his hands.

George quickly weighed the offer of a desk job, considering not only the loss of money but the loss of stature. He told the boss he "would not feel comfortable" with such an arrangement.

"I wasn't really ready to tell him to take the whole thing and shove it," George said. "So I thought for a bit and asked him about the possibility of going into sales. I was telling myself that I knew I had the ability and could still prove it."

The boss said he thought a sales position could be worked out.

"When he informed me what the position would be, I got another surprise," George said. "He told me, 'The city is yours. Go get it.' "

To an outsider that might sound like a real opportunity. What it really meant was that George would get no established accounts. He would start with nothing. That, he said, was highly irregular.

George gave the job a shot anyway. "But after I had tried it for a while," he said, "I could see that bringing a territory from a zero position was going to take too long. My base pay had been cut by half. I would have to create enough sales and gross profit to offset that base before they would start paying a commission."

George said he eventually learned that his boss had no intention of letting him get ahead in the company. "He would not admit that," George said, "but friends of mine confirmed it afterward. I felt it and they confirmed it."

On the evening of May 2, 1980, George decided to have a talk with his wife, Marlene.

"I came in from work a little beat and said, 'Dear, let me get us a drink. I've something of a serious nature to talk to you about.' Then I said, 'I'm going in there Monday and I'm going to resign.'

"She got up out of her chair, came over to me, put her arms around my neck and said, 'I thought you would never do it. They've treated you rotten for so many years. I'm just proud of you for making this decision.' "

George delivered the message to his boss on Monday. He had three weeks of vacation pay coming and asked the boss to have it mailed to him.

"I haven't spoken to him since," George said.

As it turned out, George had more than three weeks of vacation. He hadn't had any extended time off for thirteen years and decided this would be a good opportunity to get some work done around the house. He and Marlene, who also worked, were fairly well situated financially.

"So I took May, June and July off," George said. "I painted the house and did all the handyman jobs I'd never seemed to get around to before.

"I don't think I would have taken off that long if I had known then what problems a man of fifty-five would have in the job market. I felt experience was what people really wanted, and I had it. But that's not necessarily true. I got some surprises.''

THE JOB SEARCH

George had switched jobs once, when he moved west in 1960, but that was fairly easy. He'd never really had to conduct an all-out job search. After his vacation he spent a month or six weeks at it, achieving approximately nothing.

Part of the problem was his resume. (It's a common problem, and one we'll take up in detail in Chapter Seven.)

"I was referred to a company in West Los Angeles to get a resume put together for me," George said. "Somewhat after the fact I found out that the resume told too much. It was supposed to be two pages, but the man couldn't get it all in and had to put five lines on the back of one page. It was too long. It told how I went down to the big suburban store and then back to my normal job as assistant local division manager and then back down again. It looked as if I had been promoted and demoted—you know, bounced around. It was not the case, but people were reading it that way. I found out the hard way that it wasn't doing the job for me. I wasn't getting in to see anyone.''

George sent the resume to about twenty companies. He got two interviews and no offers. But "if something should come up," they said, they'd be in touch with him. Sure they would.

George decided he needed more help. Someone recommended Bernard Haldane Associates, a Boston-based career counseling firm with offices in Los Angeles, among other places. (It was through Haldane Associates that I got in touch with George. I had asked a friend at the firm, Dave Lambert, for some materials quoted elsewhere in this book. When I mentioned that I was looking for a good case study, he suggested George. I had no idea then that George and I not only had the same first name but the same distaste for December 26.)

George talked with a sales representative at Haldane Associates. "After I showed some interest," George said, "he told me he would like to talk to my wife and me together. There was going to be a cash outlay for the service: $2,200. We all talked it over, and my wife said I should go ahead if I thought this was the right approach. I said I wanted to get into the program."

As part of the program, George took a battery of tests. One was designed to measure his consistency. "They might ask the same question four times and phrase it differently each time," he said, "to see how many times you recognized something when it was written in different ways. I didn't think I did that well, but I was told there were no discrepancies in my test report."

George also had conferences with his counselor and attended a seminar. He got tips, for example, on how to handle himself at interviews.

A job-counseling service such as Haldane Associates does not actually find jobs for its clients. It does not arrange interviews for them. It is not an employment agency. Its purpose is to teach techniques that will help clients find jobs for themselves.

One of the techniques is to develop what is called a "contact network" (about which more later). The idea is to spread the word that you're looking for a job and to talk to as many contacts as possible, asking them to refer you to people who may have a job for you.

Though this technique has worked for many job hunters, George did not have much luck with it. "I got what I thought was a good referral from a friend," George said, "but it didn't pan out. They just didn't offer enough money."

George did most of his productive spadework at public libraries in La Mirada (where he lived) and nearby Norwalk.

"To start with," he said, "I spent two days looking for names of firms I thought I'd be interested in. I looked for Southern California firms as I didn't want to relocate. One of the books I used was the Dun & Bradstreet directory, and another was a Southern California business directory."

George sent letters and a new-and-improved resume to about fifty companies. That landed him about ten interviews. His counselor said that was a good percentage, but George was a little disappointed. Getting a new job was harder than he had expected.

"I felt that thirty-three years of experience, all practically with one company, and twenty years in management would be strong assets," he said. "But I found out it actually worked against me. It would come up in interviews: 'I see all your experience has been in one organization.' In other words, I hadn't had varied experience. I found out that many executives expect a person to be on the job approximately five years and then move on to other pastures. If you haven't moved, they may pull out of it that you're not motivated. It's wrong, but I know the number of years I stayed with my company worked against me."

George suspected his age also was a problem, though no one mentioned it specifically.

He had periods of depression. He was getting nowhere. He'd get down on himself.

"But then I'd think, Wait a minute. This is not the way to go. I'd sit down and do a little soul-searching and tell myself, Buddy, you're not going to make it this way, feeling sorry for yourself because you're getting turned down when you know you're good. The question is, What are you going to do about it? You can sit here and feel sorry for yourself, or you can get out and do something positive. You're the only one who can get it done. Talking to myself that way helped. That's when I'd get up and go back to the library and look up more companies I could contact. I think I almost lived in the library.

"My wife, Marlene, backed me all the way. She kept saying, 'Honey, you're too good to be kept down. The right thing is going to come along. Just keep plugging at it.' It was inspiring. She showed she had confidence in me when I was struggling. She never reflected any discouragement or criticized what I was doing."

It was at the library, in Dun & Bradstreet, that George finally found his big lead. He came across the name of a company called Republic Automotive Parts, Incorporated. It was based in Detroit but had an office in Pomona, less than an hour's drive east of Los Angeles. George wrote the president. Not long afterward, he got a call from a man in Republic's Pomona office.

"He asked if I was still looking for a job," George said, "and I said yes. He asked if I could stop by so we could sit down and talk."

George stopped by, and soon found himself being tested. "He gave me an operating statement for his unit in Pomona," George said, "and asked, 'What can you tell me about this?' I said, 'Well, what do you want to know?' And he said, 'Just anything you see there.' I said, 'Well, I see you're operating at a 3.5 percent net profit. Are you satisfied with that?' He said he wasn't and asked if I would be satisfied with it. And I said, 'Absolutely not.' Then I took his operating statement and didn't pull any punches about telling him where I thought an expense was too high. That didn't bother him. I think he just wanted to see if I could read an operating statement.

"At the end he said he'd call me in a few days. I did some research on Republic, and found they were even stronger than I had thought. I phoned the man who had interviewed me, and he told me they hadn't finalized anything yet. He put me off probably four or five times. The last time we talked, I asked him if there was any real interest in me. He said, 'Well, there very possibly could be in the near future.' I told him I thought I might be talking to the wrong man. I was told someone from headquarters would be getting in touch with me in a few days."

George had been a little assertive there. But there are times when a job applicant has to assert himself—politely—to avoid being "put on hold" by people who may be well-meaning but unable to take action on their own.

The assertiveness apparently paid off. A few days after Christmas, 1980, George got a call from the man in charge of the Boggs & McBurney Division of Republic Automotive Parts in California.

"He told me he would like to see me," George said, "and we set up an appointment for December 31, which was my fifty-sixth birthday. I spent a good part of that day with him, and along the way he tipped his hand, indicating that he intended to hire me. He had already checked me out with his counterpart at my old company. He wanted to find out why I left the company and had been told that I had a serious conflict with one individual in the company and that I was quite capable of handling the position Boggs & McBurney had in mind for me.''

And so George became a vice president and general manager of Boggs & McBurney in West Los Angeles.

He was told he could pick up a company car in the next day or two and would be on the payroll as of January 1, though he wouldn't have to report to work until January 5. In fact, if he liked, he could start off by taking a vacation. George decided that the job hadn't drained him to the point he needed a vacation just yet.

But the job search had been demanding. For more than a half year—and for the first time really in his career—George had been unemployed. And he had been actively in the hunt for a new job some three months. That's hardly an eternity as job hunts go. But when you take a vacation after leaving one job, figuring you can find another in three days or three weeks once it suits you to begin your search, three months of drawing blanks can be a real test of self-confidence. George said even his wife had become concerned near the end, though she didn't let on until after he got his new job.

One thing George discovered during his search was that he had to write off about half the day so far as job interviews were concerned.

"You're not going to get anywhere after lunch," he said. "In the afternoon, you just won't get in to see the people you want to talk to. Of all the interviews I got, I don't think more than one was after lunch. The most common time seemed to be ten o'clock.''

On reflection, it occurred to George that he himself does not give job interviews in the afternoon. "I do not think I can give a person as fair a shake as I can in the morning," he said. "You're fresher in the morning, more alert and aggressive. As the day goes along you start getting bogged down with things you have to get out of the way. I just don't set up job interviews for the afternoon. And I never set up more than two interviews a day."

When he joined Boggs & McBurney, George took over responsibility for four stores. He said his unit probably would expand by one or two stores in the next year. He was clearly excited by the prospect.

"With this company," he said, "I came out in a better position than I had the three years I was a local division manager with my old company. Just to start, my salary is about 10 percent higher. And I have more freedom in making decisions. To this point, at least, no one has second-guessed a single decision I've made."

"COME IN AND CLOSE THE DOOR"

March 1979. Abel Seller doesn't remember the exact date, but he'll never forget the scene.

Seller had been with Cole-Ossle Bargain Stores on the East Coast for almost twenty years, rising from sales clerk to advertising manager of the store's big-volume major appliances department. Now, by invitation, he entered his boss's office.

"Come in and close the door," the boss said.

As it turned out, the boss was the one who would close the door—on Seller's career at Cole-Ossle. But let's hear the story from Seller himself, after a brief pause for character identification.

(While the story is true, Seller's name is not. Nor are the names of the companies involved. As we shall see, Seller would again become part of a circle of business people he knew while at Cole-Ossle. It was a harmonious circle in which even direct competitors were on reasonably good terms. Seller did not want to disturb that harmony by starting an argument over how he was treated at Cole-Ossle. Hence the assumed names.)

Here, distilled from his written recollections and an extended interview, is Seller's own account of his downfall, and his eventual resurgence:

I'd been out a couple of days, in bed with a fever, when I got a call saying the boss wanted to see me the next day. I had to get out of a sick bed to make the meeting, but I was really excited. I was sure I was going to get a promotion, or at least an increase in salary. My division of the store had really leaped ahead. We had gone into a third branch expansion, and I thought I'd done my share to make it possible. (As a matter of fact, much of what I had done in major promotion language and ad layout is being used by the store to this day. That, I think, is quite a compliment.)

Anyway, when I got the call, I told myself, Boy, this is terrific!

It wasn't terrific.

No sooner had the boss told me to come in and close the door than he said, "We have to discuss your termination."

"Termination?" I said. "You mean fired?" I went absolutely limp.

The last thing in the world I expected was a dismissal notice. I was heading for my twentieth anniversary and had spent the last eleven years as advertising manager for a big department in a world-famous store. I thought we'd had one of our best years. It just didn't make sense.

Well, the boss said reassuringly, "fired" was a harsh word, and that wasn't exactly it. There comes a time, he said, when a business moves on and people outgrow jobs or jobs outgrow people. My ability to handle "the changing nature of the business" had been questioned. The boss said I was entitled to a sixty-day trial during which I would have a chance to prove my worth by handling some "special" projects. But in the next breath he suggested I might be happier if I resigned and sought employment elsewhere.

Then came a barrage of superlatives describing my sterling character, delightful personality and many business attributes that would make me a real asset to a new employer. I had to ask myself a question at that point: If I'm all that good, why the hell doesn't my present employer want me?

I remember thinking about a school play in which I had the lead. It was Arthur Miller's *Death of a Salesman*. I was Willie Loman. Now, twenty-odd years later, I could still hear him crying out, "You can't eat the orange and throw the peel away. . . . A man is not a piece of fruit!" Not until this moment had I truly felt Willie's anguish and emptiness. I was alone and lost.

How could my life have become such a disaster so suddenly? What would I say to my advertising staff? They were more than employees. They were friends. Would they still respect me? How could I explain my failure to my two sons, my former wife, my mother and my fiancee? They'd all been proud of me.

I found a phone and called my fiancee.

"I've been bad," I began.

It's interesting I would have put it that way. I think it's because we equate "fired" with "bad." I'd been called in and told I failed. So, for the moment, at least, I guess I thought I must have done something bad.

You're just not prepared when something like that happens. It's not taught in school. No one tells you to expect that someday someone might say, "We're firing you." I think it would be a good thing to acquaint people with the possibility. You may be fired without good reason, and you should be prepared to pick yourself up and move on.

A friend of mine knew a guy in his forties, an engineer, who lost his job. It could have been in one of those defense industry cutbacks. He had a beautiful home, two cars, children. He was a successful guy. After he was let out, he began looking for any kind of work. He even tried to find openings for counter help in restaurants. He was overqualified for every job he tried for.

One night his wife came home and found him in his chair. She thought he was sleeping. He was, and it would be a long sleep. He was dead. The doctors said it was basically anguish. The cause of death was heart failure, but he had no history of heart problems. I guess he died of a broken heart.

It never occurred to me that I couldn't go on. I'm not a quitter. But I was shocked, puzzled.

My fiancee (now my wife) was very supportive. On the phone, when I told her I'd been fired, she reacted as if I'd just pulled off a brilliant maneuver. "Oh, that's wonderful!" she said. "Let's have a champagne brunch to celebrate."

As we talked, over our eggs Benedict and Dom Perignon, she reminded me that I hadn't really been happy with the job the past two years. I had been fighting a losing battle to be included in decision-making meetings involving expansion into the suburbs. What I was really looking for was a promotion from advertising manager to promotions director of my department. The department was such an important part of the store that it occupied an entire floor, and we often got whole newspaper ads to ourselves. With the store planning expansions, I saw an opening for a person who would supervise promotion for appliance departments at all the branches. As promotions director, I would be a step above advertising director and would be in overall charge of all radio and TV advertising and all advertising displays in the store and in newspapers. I would report to a senior promotions director with storewide authority. I had been assured by a former boss that my "big break" would come with expansion. Now we were expanding but the break wasn't coming. The store was growing, and so was my resentment. Nothing ever came of my pitch to become a promotions director.

I would get calls from my vice president–boss and the storewide advertising director. Without explanation, they would request information about my department and copies of ads from my files. It was quite upsetting to learn later that they were preparing presentations for top-level management, using my materials but not my name. They would not let me become visible to top management as a planner and responsible executive.

Now, after my "termination" meeting, it was clear they didn't even want me around as an invisible department advertising director. I'm still not sure why they were replacing me. I think basically it was that the store president thought the person in charge of a growing department like mine should have experience in overall promotion and not just a background in department advertising. It wasn't expressed exactly that way, but that's what I got out of it.

When I returned to the store a few days later, having recovered from my fever if not the termination notice, I was greeted by a dozen well-wishers who wanted to say goodbye. Some had heard I quit, others that I was fired. That was strange. I had said nothing to anyone at the store. I hadn't even told my boss whether I would look elsewhere, as he suggested, or take the sixty-day trial I had been offered.

I spent the next two weeks in limbo, waiting for somebody to come in and say, "Would you please get out of here tomorrow." Nobody did. I tried to call my boss several times but couldn't get through to him. So I called the head of personnel. I knew him pretty well. I told him I'd been fired and wanted to find out what I was supposed to do.

"What do you mean you were fired?" he asked. "You'd better come up and talk to me."

He said he thought I had jumped to a conclusion. I said, "If somebody told you to sit down and talk about your termination, what would you think?" He said he thought my boss had screwed it up and didn't mean to say termination. The store would never treat a dedicated executive in such a shoddy manner. "We will work with you on an intensive sixty-day study program to see if you prove worthy of the next step up the ladder," he said. But I could resign if I felt I was being treated unfairly.

LIBERATION

I decided to resign. I was told I would see the personnel director's boss. He said I was being hasty. The store would never fire such an exemplary person. But it was true, he said, that somebody was taking over my job. He would also take over my desk, in front of all the people who had been reporting to me. He would be my boss.

"It could be a wonderful learning experience," I was told. "Yes," I said, "I'm certainly learning more and more by the minute." It was the old squeeze play.

Within two months of the "termination" meeting at which I was not fired, I left Cole-Ossle.

The person who replaced me lasted three months. About the time he left, the company president rather suddenly "resigned."

My fiancee had assured me that any failure was theirs, not mine. I finally came to realize she was right. She was not just trying to be helpful. She was being truthful.

Anyway, my leaving Cole-Ossle was the end of a long relationship I'd started as a $49-a-week sales clerk. I'd moved up from that job to a minor supervisory position. I later transferred to the advertising department and became a junior copywriter, then a senior copywriter, then assistant advertising manager and finally advertising manager.

It was odd the way it had started. When I took the first job at the store, I wasn't planning to stay. I had no business training. I had attended a private college, majoring in general education, which prepares you for nothing. Then I went to a dramatics school. It specialized in radio, television and theater arts. I was hoping to get some kind of a performing job, whether acting on stage or doing radio announcing. I spent two years studying and thought I had potential.

Then I did a six-month tour of duty in the Army Reserve.

DECEMBER 26 REVISITED / 89

When I got out, I was hoping to contact a family friend who was influential in the theater, thinking he might get me in a stock theater company in New York. But he was in Europe when I came back from the army. So I decided to take a job to tide myself over until something came up in the theater or broadcasting or whatever. That's how I got started at Cole-Ossle.

To my surprise, I found that I enjoyed the work. I gave up the idea of a career in broadcasting or dramatics. By the time I was fifty, I thought, maybe I'd be a store vice-president. They kept telling me the sky was the limit.

When the sky finally fell in and I left Cole-Ossle, my fiancee and I kicked around many ideas, some reasonably good, a few pretty far out. Particularly dear was her suggestion that she give up her life's dream of a career in opera so we could buy a pig farm. After a few more preposterous possibilities, we decided my immediate need was not for a job but for a vacation. And so it was that I enjoyed a spring and summer as I had no other since my childhood. Then, well rested and feeling a lot better about myself, I decided to try to make a living at what had been a twenty-year hobby: photography. I read every photography book I could get my hands on, and there were dozens. I joined a camera club with a studio and darkroom facilities. I enrolled in two night-school photography courses at a famous local university. Then I formed a one-man photography business.

What I enjoyed most was art photography. I did both black-and-white and color, mostly of waterfront scenes and other local landmarks. At a friend's suggestion, I approached one of the galleries about displaying some of my work. The gallery carried a minimum of photographs, but the person I talked to there was encouraging. I showed him a black-and-white photo —I think it was of a tall ship. I had no idea what it was worth. "What would you get for something like this?" I asked. "Five bucks?" He said maybe thirty or thirty-five. I think he sold it for around eighty. Gee, I thought, I must not be that bad. Maybe even pretty good.

I also had pictures on display at one of the stores in town. A woman contacted the store and said she wanted to buy some of my work. I showed her some snaps. "What are you going to do with these pictures?" I asked. "I'm an amateur photographer," she said, "and when I saw your work I just wanted to buy some of your pictures to use as examples of perfection." She bought about a dozen 8-by-10 prints.

I was having fun. But I wasn't selling enough pictures to make a good living. I was in the business about a year and a half. Then I heard from a friend that a fellow I had known in retailing was looking for me. We finally found each other, and he said he was in the process of going into his own business. It would be similar to the line of business I'd been in with Cole-Ossle, and it would be in the same geographic area. He wanted to know if I'd be interested in coming in as a principal employee who would be in charge of all his promotion. I fell instantly apart. This was a person I respected. "Count me in," I said.

That's how I came to join Stu Pendice Discounts, Incorporated. We sell brand-name merchandise at discount prices. I came in as promotions director—the very job I'd wanted and couldn't get at Cole-Ossle.

The new job really made a tremendous difference in my life. My wife noticed. My children noticed. It was a lot of work but I loved it. I'm not sure how many hours I put in during an average week (sometimes I'm working even when I'm sitting at home), but I probably spend fifty to sixty hours a week in the store.

It's as though I've picked up six or seven years in terms of salary advancement. I'm making nearly twice what I was at Cole-Ossle.

I have never worked as many hours or as hard as I do now, and have never been so happy about a job.

5 / Coming Back: Game Plan

FIRST: SHAPE UP

Maybe you haven't been as lucky as George Stocks and Abel Seller. You've shared half their experience by losing a job, but you haven't shared the second half by finding a new one. The next order of business, obviously, is to devise a game plan that will make you a big second-half performer.

If you've been disemployed and are looking for a solution instead of a place to hide, you're already on the right track. You've already taken the offensive. And maybe the game plan you're following is as good as any I could suggest. I can't certify that the steps I'm about to recommend are foolproof, but I can assure you they are not just ideas I pulled out of the air to get a chapter written. I've been fired more times than Wyatt Earp's pistol—or at least that's the way it feels—and I think I've learned some rules others might profitably apply.

If it hasn't already, it may strike you as you read on that I am sometimes preoccupied with small matters. It has been my observation that big things are usually made of a lot of little things.

91

Rule: If you are to accomplish big things, you must organize the small tasks of which great things are made.

Anyway, here's the plan:

Get in Shape. I suspect that surprises you. It may seem to have nothing to do with finding a new job. But I think it's about the most valuable advice I can offer.

Find yourself a place to run; or, if you can't stand running, choose another form of exercise. But get in shape. Good health is always an asset, but right now it's about the best thing you can have going for you.

A woman who teaches high school said that at the beginning of her health course she asks her class to list the five things most needed for a happy life. The students typically list things like "a new Firebird," "a beautiful wife" (or "good-looking husband") and "a high-paying job." Some of the more perceptive add such things as "a good education," "love" and "recognition." Few recognize the value of good health. They take it for granted.

The ancients knew what they were doing when they developed the ideal of a sound mind in a sound body. Most modern educators and other authorities agree that ability to function at optimal level mentally depends to a great extent on physical well-being.

Exercise is excellent therapy for depression. When you're down emotionally, you tend to go down physically, too. Just thinking about your problems can wear you out, both mentally and physically. I woke up exhausted every morning for days after I was fired. I had to fight the urge to turn over in bed and go back to sleep. To increase my strength, I ran and did other exercises. And I forced myself to do my running in the morning. I knew I'd stay in bed half the day if I didn't apply pressure on myself to get moving.

Jogging or running not only improves your cardiorespiratory efficiency but also makes you aware of your body. You are forced to concentrate on your physical being, and this takes up time that might otherwise be spent brooding. Many joggers say running is a cathartic for worry. They find it impossible to stay depressed while exercising. This may not be true for all people at all times, but it certainly is in many cases, mine included.

I've always believed exercise is valuable for athletes and non-athletes alike. I'm not an athlete, but I know I feel better after exercising. When I left the Redskins in 1978, jogging took on a new meaning in my life. As I ran more and more, working myself up to from three to six miles a day, I began to view the accomplishment as a new assertion of myself. It was a time when I really needed that kind of lift. Coaching had taxed me to my limits, both physically and mentally, but had also filled my day and furnished many gratifying moments. Now I had no job. Exercising helped fill the void, and diverted my attention from the negative aspects of life.

I've found that morning exercise creates a good pace and mood for the day. I'm a tense person. Without some kind of release, a tense person is soon apt to become a past-tense person. But exercise relaxes me. I've discovered that when I get tied up on the phone all day, or become so involved in other tasks that I have to skip my daily exercising, I have trouble sleeping at night.

It's easy to fit running or other exercise into your daily schedule if you accept the notion that it's really good for you. Until you do accept it, though, you'll find a thousand excuses for not working out. The best way to attack this problem is to make exercising your first daily priority. Work out early. Then you'll have the rest of the day to attack your other problems—and more strength and stamina to attack them with.

Job hunting is an emotional experience. But it can also drain you physically. Anxiety and depression can sap your strength even if you've just been sitting at a desk all day. Daily exercise can give you the physical strength you need to meet emotional demands.

I started running from my home in Palos Verdes Estates to Rolling Hills High School (aptly named, as I soon discovered). I'd run a couple of laps around the school track, do one hundred or more situps and a few stretching exercises, then run back home. I tried to follow the same command I'd often given my players: Make an extra effort. If I had set out to do one hundred situps, I'd make a point of doing at least one extra, in case I'd miscounted. If I had planned to run four miles, I'd try for four and one-quarter. The hills in my neighborhood are pretty steep, and whenever I'd feel like stopping I'd tell myself, Just one more telephone pole, George. You can make *one* more pole! Then I'd urge myself to the next pole, and the next, until I'd accomplished my goal, plus a little extra. I'm not telling you this to show what a disciplined fellow I am. Others have daily regimens just as hard, and harder. My purpose is to show how mental toughness is developed. Only one person can make you mentally tough: you.

I told a reporter once, "Sometimes I'll walk along the beach and pick up rocks and throw them in the ocean. If one is tucked in the sand and bigger than I thought, I won't just leave it there and keep walking. I'll dig it out. I won't let that rock defeat me."[1]

The rock of course was of no importance in itself. It was worth no more than the sand it was stuck in. I was just going through a little training exercise. Sticking to small tasks like that can help train you to be mentally tough.

Staying with an exercise program, and expanding it, can serve the same purpose. It is also a valuable first step toward restructuring your life after a serious setback of any kind. So jog, if you are able. If not, swim. Take long walks. Bowl. Play golf or tennis. Ride a bicycle. Go dancing or skating.

You should of course consult a doctor as to the type and amount of exercise you can safely undertake. Strenuous exercise can be dangerous, even fatal, if your body is not prepared for it. If you start a jogging program, don't plan on covering three miles a day for openers.

Two more health tips for the unemployed:

This is a time when you may be tempted to drink excessively. Don't. It can impair both your physical and mental health, and it can't get you another job, unless there's an opening somewhere for town drunk. If you have a question about whether you're drinking too much, you might take a little test I came across in a newspaper:

Do you ever stay home from work because of drinking? Is drinking causing trouble in your family? Do you have blackouts (loss of memory of events that happened or of your actions while drinking)? Have you lost a job or business because of drinking? Do you have to keep on drinking once you have started? Has a doctor ever treated you for drinking-induced problems (liver or stomach trouble, accidents, etc.)? Do you need to have a drink at a certain time every day? Do you drink too much at the wrong times (weddings, important social occasions)? Do you wish you could quit drinking and can't? Have you had an accident because of drinking? Have you ever been arrested because of drunk driving? Has drinking affected your health and family life? Do you feel guilty after drinking? Does your family want you to stop drinking? If you stopped drinking, would your life become more manageable?

And, beneath the quiz, these scoring instructions:

If you answered yes to one question: A warning!
Two yes answers: You are an alcoholic![2]

The second tip is to stay away from the refrigerator between meals, unless that's where you keep your job-application forms. Gaining weight, as I said earlier, can hurt your chances of landing another job. The effect on your health can be even more harmful.

Get Out of the House. You may remember my story about being invited to a Friars' Club dinner and not wanting to go because I was embarrassed to be seen in public after being fired. You'll discover, as I did, that it's good to get out. People will think more of you, not less. I mean that two ways. They'll admire you more for not hiding, and they'll think about you more because you're visible. Who knows? An acquaintance may have heard of a job opening but may never think to tell you about it if he never sees you. Don't hibernate. Circulate.

As one writer put it in an article on dealing with unemployment, "the key ingredient is purposeful action." The writer offered this guidance from psychiatrist Martin Goldberg, director of marital therapy at the Institute of Pennsylvania Hospital in Philadelphia:

"The worst thing to do when you're unemployed is to do nothing. Anything that keeps you active mentally and physically, that keeps your skills in shape, that sharpens them or adds new skills, is worthwhile. Unless you're doing some constructive work at home, don't be at home. Be *out*, whether it's for formal job seeking or meeting with friends or going to classes, because your next opportunity is in the outer world somewhere—not within the four walls of your apartment or house."

A colleague of Dr. Goldberg's, psychiatrist Paul Dormont, elaborated on the theme:

"It's important for anyone who is out of work not to take the attitude that 'I don't want to see friends because I'm ashamed of being unemployed.' Any decent friend is going to be sympathetic and understanding and, if apprised of the situation, can be on the lookout for a job opening. In many instances it's only by word of mouth that the existence of jobs gets known."[3]

Do Things You Really Don't Want to Do. This is a broader application of the first two suggestions. Besides forcing yourself to exercise and to get out of the house, force yourself to fill the rest of the day with productive pursuits. They may involve both work and relaxation. But include some of those things you should have done weeks or months ago but have been avoiding. Put them on that daily schedule we were talking about earlier.

When you were employed, there were times you just didn't feel like getting up in the morning and dragging yourself off to the office or plant. But you did it anyway. You had to. It was expected of you. And it kept you disciplined. Unemployed, you must try to develop the same kind of discipline, to keep yourself busy. Looking for work probably won't keep you occupied full-time. There may be days when you have no job interviews and few leads to follow. Fill up the time. You could take on one of those home-repair jobs you've been ducking. The magazine article quoted a few paragraphs back recommended this as good psychological medicine: "If worked on cooperatively, these projects might have a unifying effect on a family; if undertaken alone, the sense of accomplishment will help lift the unemployed person's self-esteem."

If you can't find anything useful to do at home, you might volunteer some of your spare time to community-service projects. Or you might stuff envelopes for a political candidate of your choice—and maybe keep him or her from becoming disemployed. Anytime you do something you'd just as soon not do, you develop a little more self-discipline. That's a good investment in itself. And if what you do is worthwhile, you get a second dividend.

Helping others is not really selfless activity. It makes you feel so good, you're actually helping yourself. You're doing it for you as well as for them. I have served as chairman of the Summer Jobs for Needy Youth Program for nine years, have been director of the Myasthenia Gravis Foundation and Multiple Sclerosis Foundation, have established two scholarship funds at Gallaudet College, a school for the deaf in Washington, and one at Morningside College, where I once coached. I've worked for the Sioux Indians and the Land of the Red Cloud in Pine Ridge, South Dakota. And they've all done at least as much for me as I have for them.

Helping others can be especially helpful to you when you're unemployed. It takes your mind off your own problems. When you're helping the really unfortunate, you won't think about yourself. Or, if you do, you'll realize you're luckier than you thought.

Analyze Yourself. A recent study showed that three-fourths of all teenagers are fired from their first jobs within three months. The most common reason is that they can't get along with their bosses. It's not that they can't do the work.

Is there a negative element in your own personality? In coaching, you can be the all-time master of Xs and Os and still not win consistently if you can't relate to your players. I think it's that way in most jobs.

A young man complained recently that he was not the kind of person other people thought he was. "People react to me as being a friendly but independent sort of person," he said. "Girls like being around me, I guess, but they don't seem to want to get close to me. Every time I meet a girl I could really go for, she treats me like her brother. But I'm not independent, and I don't want to be anybody's big brother. I want to be loved and needed."

A friend steered the young man to a book called *Body Language*.[4] It describes nonverbal ways in which we communicate with those around us.

If the way you see yourself does not jibe with the way others see you, you may be unconsciously projecting an image that can adversely affect you. And it may be that you should not only analyze yourself but let a professional analyst have a go at it as well.

Make at Least One Effort a Day to Get a Job. You may have been wondering when I would get around to talking about actually going after a job. I haven't overlooked this rather important phase of your mission, but I'm still not quite ready to go into job-hunting techniques in detail. That will come a little later. The point I want to make here is that you should gear yourself mentally for the hunt. Resolve now, at the general planning stage, to make at least one positive effort a day to find a job. And don't let yourself forget the resolution. It might even be a good idea to put it in writing.

Persistence will be the idea. Sometimes, if you're lucky, opportunity will knock at your door. Better that you should keep knocking at opportunity's door.

SWITCHING JOBS

You also need a game plan if you're thinking of moving into a different job field. This is true whether you're out of work and looking for a new line or on the job and anxious to get away from it and into something else.

If you happen to be disemployed, right about now would be an ideal occasion for a searching analysis of what you really want to do with the rest of your work life. A sound analysis takes time, and time is one thing you've got in good supply.

Up until my last firing, at least, I never thought about changing jobs. I always loved coaching. Some coaches say they love the work because they can be like kids and keep playing long after their peers have grown up. I've never seen it that way. To me, coaching was more than just playing a game. It was a way of life. I loved the competition, the challenge, the relations with players. At Washington, my relationship with the players, the entire Redskin organization and the city of Washington was something really special to me.

But I have no quarrel with other coaches whose motivation is different, so long as they love their work. I think that's the key. If you love your work, it's really no longer work. I can think of no prospect more appealing than waking up every morning looking forward to the day's work, and none more appalling than having to face a job you hate.

In a five-year survey conducted at a rural southern high school, more than 85 percent of the seniors said they did not want to go into agriculture-related business after graduation. Yet 85 percent of them wound up working in either agriculture or agri-business. It is hardly surprising to hear complaints about apathy of young adults in that community. It's hard to get excited about a job you perceive to be leading nowhere.

I was luckier. I worked at many different jobs (at one time or another I was a caddy, an office boy, a yard worker, a firewood chopper, a dishwashing machine operator, a potato peeler, a floor mopper, a table waiter, a soda jerk, a strawberry picker, an apple picker, a cherry picker, a window washer, a playground director, a camp counselor, a camp director, a lifeguard, a postal worker, a car-wash employee, a grocery clerk, a hat checker, a boxcar unloader, a snow shoveler, a basement cleaner, a magazine seller, a gas station attendant, a delivery boy, a glass-washing machine operator, a Ditto machine operator, an elevator operator and a coach or teacher of basketball, baseball, volleyball, track and field, golf, tennis, badminton, weight training, swimming and archery, among other things), but there was never a doubt in my mind about a career. I always wanted to be a football coach.

As a result, I was able to focus my energies on learning my profession when the time came. At one point early in my coaching career, I tried selling life insurance, and went so far as to enroll in insurance school and become licensed. But I gave it up. It was taking too much time away from coaching. It showed me a lesson: If you try to divide your time between two major enterprises, you will reduce your effectiveness at both.

If you can't stand the kind of work you're doing (or were doing before you got fired), and you're sure the problem is traceable to the job and not you, by all means try to find another field.

But make a careful study before you make a move. Don't go after a job because it looked glamorous when you saw someone doing it in a movie or magazine ad.

Coaching, for example, may strike you as a glamorous profession. But if you got into it, you might hate it. An obvious way to get a reading on a job is to talk to people who have worked at it. But don't just talk. Size them up. If they appear similar to you in temperament, and they all look bored, have a second thought.

I understand, of course, that you may not always have a lot of choices. As this is written, we live in anything but a job-hunter's market. When jobs are hard to come by, and good ones practically impossible to find, the best job may be the one you can get (or the one you already have). Football coaches are acutely aware of this. Many former head coaches in the National Football League have become assistant coaches because that was the best they could do if they wanted to stay in the game.

Some people, of course, don't want to stay in the same game. A Canadian magazine article on working women suggested the number of such people is growing:

"Changing careers in midstream is no longer the highly exceptional move it used to be. Allison Roberts, acting director of the Ontario Ministry of Labor's Women's Bureau, says, 'Many women are realizing that they will spend an average of twenty-five years in the paid work force. In response, many are switching to careers in nontraditional areas which will allow greater job satisfaction and higher pay.' "[5]

The article cited the experience of Joanne Emslie, who quit her job as a high school German and French teacher to become an international marketing consultant. "Her career change was meticulously planned," the article said. "Emslie knew she wanted to travel and make use of her languages. . . . She attended Project Link, a two-weekend career-change seminar designed for teachers. Here she learned how to write resumes and prepare for job interviews. Four months later she had what she wanted."

The article also mentioned the case of Kathleen Christie, a "burned-out" social worker who—with careful planning—made a successful career switch:

"I decided, over about a six-month period, to make a total change," Christie said. "I pinpointed what my strengths and capabilities were, which ones an organization would want to buy, identified jobs I liked and which ones were available, and then talked to different people about these jobs. I looked at a whole range of personnel-related jobs. Then I went out knocking on doors and within a few months I sold myself on my interpersonal skills as a management consultant."

A somewhat similar article in the *Oakland Tribune* said people who had made successful mid-career changes reported that they could not have done it without "planning, financial and moral support and, perhaps most of all, hard work to make the dream a reality."[6]

One of several brief case studies in the article told of the transformation of Avi Stachenfeld from lawyer to filmmaker. "Stachenfeld . . . graduated from Harvard Law School in 1968. He moved to San Francisco that same year and practiced nearly a decade before deciding he preferred visual media to legal language. He enrolled in the UC-Berkeley master's program in journalism in 1974. While he was a student, he spent a summer in Salinas filming his first documentary, about union organizing among California farm workers. The ten-minute documentary, *Fruits of Labor,* he said, surprised him by winning several awards.''

He eventually started his own production company, making political and artistic documentaries, commercials and industrial training films. Through a subsidiary company, he kept a finger in the law, filming pretrial testimony of witnesses in lawsuits.

"Transitions are always hard to talk about," Stachenfeld said, "but my change of direction was less difficult because I knew that my talents lay elsewhere than in the law."

The change, he said, was a real release. It was once a grind to work from nine to five, he said, but now "two o'clock is no different from seven o'clock."

Then there was the case of Marty Mallory, who turned her attention from the money temple to the choir loft.

After working eleven years for a bank, the *Oakland Tribune* story said, Mallory asked herself if that was what she wanted to do the rest of her life. The answer: "I had never wanted to be in banking in the first place, and I decided I wasn't going to work there any more."

Upshot: As the *Tribune* story was about to appear, Mallory was packing for a trip to Minnesota, where she had been accepted by a Bible college offering a major in sacred music.

"I don't know why it took so long for me to find something I really want to do," she said. "I didn't finish college because I got married and I joined the bank because I had to work. So it just never occurred to me until now that you could make a living doing something you liked."

In an earlier chapter I mentioned the problem women face if they decide to go into the job market after years of homemaking. As I suggested, it can be a really difficult transition. But some women have carried it off amazingly well. Consider this success story:

"Madelon Talley manages thirty persons and some $13 billion as head of the New York State Retirement Fund. . . . Twelve years ago she was a thirty-six-year-old housewife whose management duties revolved around her home and three children. Talley is one of many women who are a little-noted but growing phenomenon in the business world—'late bloomers' who have enjoyed unusually rapid career success after careers as homemakers.

"A vice president of a multinational bank, personnel director of a major manufacturing company, senior vice president of the world's largest advertising agency and scores of executives in nearly every kind of occupation belong to this select group. Many did not even enter college until their own children were in school.'' [7]

One of the heroines of the story was Rena Bartos, who spent ten years raising a family, then returned to a career in market research and became a senior vice president of the J. Walter Thompson advertising agency. She said the time she spent at home actually helped her:

"Those years were the most rewarding of my life in terms of personal development. And I found that maturity was a real advantage. Coming back I could see how much the agency functioned just like the PTA. And I developed what I called the 'Dr. Spock Theory' of advertising: Dealing with some of the more explosive executives is much like talking to a three-year-old having a tantrum; you've learned to be calm, consistent, to stand your ground.''

Such success stories are of course not common. Otherwise, people wouldn't be turning them into magazine articles. Generally, as you get older, switching careers gets harder. This is true not only of homemakers but of older men who find they still need work after the company no longer needs them. Some of these men have success stories, too, as related by an author of my acquaintance:

"I have an older brother, John, who, as the result of his boss's son graduating from college and taking over his advertising job, was forcibly 'retired' when he was in his early sixties. He had little in the way of financial reserves, so he moved to a comparatively inexpensive locality in Florida and started to try to scratch around for a living. For quite a long time things did not go well and he had severe money troubles. . . . Then, one day, John 'invented' a job.

"As an advertising man, he knew a good deal about printing. He found a job printer in his locality and explained his idea to him. . . . John's idea was to establish himself as a 'printing consultant,' and to be the liaison between a company that required any printing work to be done and the printer. . . . He had his own car, and so could act as a daily go-between, taking orders from a business concern, delivering them the same day to the printer, and picking up and delivering by hand when the work was ready. For these services, valuable to both parties, he received a commission on the cost of the job done. . . .

"He's active, happy in this new undertaking, and is making out very nicely in a brand new career that he invented when he was nearing seventy years of age. My brother John hung in there wonderfully when the going seemed to be hopeless. I'm grateful that we have the same genes."[8]

Not everyone will have the tools John had to work with, let alone the resourcefulness he displayed in putting them to use. If you think a job change is imperative, and can identify a field you're sure you'd like, you might consider taking an entry-level position. The pay is almost guaranteed to be low. But if you love soup and can't stand nuts, better to be a label licker in a soup cannery than a foreman in a nut factory. In the soup cannery, you might eventually move up to chief canner. In the nut factory, you'll wind up a filbert.

Again, however, have a look before you leap. And try not to leap too often. The author of a *Money* magazine article aimed at executives (but probably applicable to many nonexecutives as well) had this to say of chronic job hopping:

"It can help people in the early stages of their careers acquire valuable training and experience, as well as sharpen their goals. Eventually, however, an executive who becomes hooked on hopping pays a heavy price. . . . Prospective employers may regard the overly mobile manager as an opportunist whose services are available to the highest bidder. They may conclude that he cannot get along with coworkers. Or they may question whether he will stay long enough to finish a job. Contends Janet Jones-Parker, chairman of Boyden/Management Woman, a recruiting firm in Greenwich, Connecticut: 'If you've moved four times in twelve years, that's too many. You've got to stay long enough to demonstrate that you've accomplished something.' That could take five years or so.''[9]

Still, the article said, there are times when the general rule against job hopping should be disregarded. In some fields, such as advertising, consumer-products marketing, fashion design, publishing and retailing, frequent job changes are the norm.

But one researcher who studied the migratory habits of presidents of five hundred of the country's largest companies found that most didn't migrate at all. Since 1953, the study showed, more than half had been one-company men.

"Even executive recruiters, who have the most to gain by increased mobility among managers, acknowledge that job hopping should be a last resort," the *Money* magazine report said. "Says J. Gerald Simmons, president of the New York City–based Handy Associates: 'The surest way to become president of a company is to go with the firm when you get out of college and stay with it.' "

If you're thinking of changing fields, or jobs within a field, you might consider these tips from a professional:

"Don't change jobs for money alone. Many people think they would be happier in another position that paid more money. They look for an identical job at a higher salary. . . . Unfortunately, money will buy many things but not job satisfaction. . . . Such things as lack of opportunity for advancement should be the basis for a decision. . . .

"Don't change jobs when you feel you're over your head. Being somewhat insecure . . . in your position is a healthy sign that you have growing room. By working harder to overcome your lack of knowledge or experience you should be able to overcome such feelings of inadequacy. Not having all the answers is not a reason in itself to switch positions. . . .

"Don't change jobs when you can't get along with your co-workers. Having a new position is no guarantee there won't be any personality conflicts. . . .

"Don't change jobs on a low note. . . . The time to change jobs is when you're on top, not when you're on your way out. . . . Go out as a champion. . . . [Then] you'll know you're not just running away from your old position because you couldn't cut it.

"Don't change jobs because you're bored. It could be all you need is just a vacation. Two weeks away from the office has done wonders for frustrated executives who thought what they needed was a new job. You'll bring back . . . new perspectives and ideas which might light a fire under you. If that doesn't work, try asking for more responsibilities. If that doesn't work either, then you're not being challenged mentally. There's a big difference between that and just being bored.

"Finally, don't change jobs before you have a firm offer in writing."[10]

So much for when not to change jobs. On the flip side, consider these observations by Barry F. Nathanson, president of Richards Consultants, Limited, a New York executive-search firm:

"Most people really don't focus on whether their job has good prospects—at least not as much as they should. They need to be more alert in recognizing the warning signals of a dead-end job."

Among those signals: "You should be concerned if your superior is not well regarded within the corporate structure or if he or she is someone who is not slated to move up. That lack of progress could in turn block your chances of advancement."

On being passed over for a promotion: "It shouldn't be taken too seriously if an individual has been on the job for a short period . . . and the company decides to go to the outside for someone with significantly more experience. [But] if the company brings in somebody with the same amount of expertise at much more money, then the message for those passed over is not at all subtle."

On how often a person "on the way up" should expect a promotion: "In some companies, if you haven't had a promotion in eighteen months, you're not a fast-track individual. In others, three years in the same position is fine. In the Big Eight accounting firms, you may have to be on the job twelve to fifteen years before being considered as a partner.''

On what a prospective employee should look for: "To insure that one's job does have a future, workers should be looking at a company's sales record, market share and commitment to new products and opportunities: Is the firm merely content to rest on its laurels? What is its five-year plan? Too often, people don't ask those questions until after they've taken the job.''[11]

If you do decide a job change is in order, don't use your departure as an occasion to unload on the boss you're leaving behind. I always avoided loud exits. Slamming the door behind you could close doors ahead of you. If you'd like to hear it from a second source, listen to Bruce J. Robertson, president of the executive-recruiting firm of Smyth Dawson Associates in New York:

"Time and time again I have come across situations that show the value of an amicable parting between employee and boss. The person who quits in a huff and cuts off all ties to a former employer probably will live to regret it. By contrast, the man or woman who leaves a job graciously and with dignity has a couple of advantages. . . .

"First, the former employer will be far more willing to provide a good reference at a later time. Second, it's quite possible that the person who is leaving will be considered for another—and better—position with his old firm some time in the future. I know of several instances where an individual left on friendly terms with the boss and was invited back a year or so later to a more important post. . . .

"I recall the case of one middle-aged man . . . who resigned from a marketing job and took a new one in a different city. He left under the best of circumstances. Six months later [his] previous boss, a vice president, was brought in at that same level by the new company. So his old boss became his new boss. . . . The arrival of his former superior at the new company worked out to his advantage.''[12]

By contrast, Robertson cited the case of a young executive

who left some ears burning at his old company when he got an offer from another corporation. As it turned out, he also burned a bridge in front of him. His employer-to-be was making a final check of his references when he learned of his stormy exit from his old firm and withdrew the job offer.

Robertson suggested following these basic rules when leaving a job:

"Make it clear that your resignation is the result of a firm offer from another employer. Right up to your last minute on the job, provide cooperative and intelligent workmanship. If you're asked to break in the person who might be succeeding you, offer . . . genuine assistance. . . . Don't breach any confidences you have held. Clear up any financial debts you may have and return all company property. . . . Two weeks' notice is standard procedure, but, if you can, give the company you are leaving additional time. Don't bad-mouth, in your new organization, the company you have left."

1. Alfred Wright, "You Win! You're Fired!" *Sports Illustrated*, September 7, 1970.
2. Vicki Alexander, "Alcoholism Recovery Service Families Fight Back Together," South Bay Examiner Supplement, *Los Angeles Herald Examiner*, November 5, 1981.
3. Maxine Schnall, "How to Weather Unemployment," *Woman's Day*, October 14, 1980.
4. Julius Fast, *Body Language* (New York: M. Evans & Co., 1970).
5. Peggy McCallum, "Career Switching: How to Quit & Win," *Chatelaine*, February 1981.
6. Bethany Korwin-Pawlowska, "Going Through Those Changes: Finding the Right Career Takes Time," *Oakland Tribune*, August 24, 1981.
7. Eleanor Berman, "Home-Grown Executives," *American Way*, May 1981.
8. Peter Schwed, *Hanging in There* (Boston: Houghton Mifflin, 1977).
9. Malcolm N. Carter, "Careers: The Ins and Outs of Switching Jobs," *Money*, October 1981.
10. Jack M. Polizzi, president, Wells Management Corporation, Agency Division, "On the Job Front," *New York Post*, June 2, 1980.
11. "Trapped in a Dead-End Job?" *U.S. News & World Report*, June 1, 1981.
12. "Quitting a Job—How to Do It With Style," *U.S. News & World Report*, February 2, 1981.

6 / Never Again

DEFENSIVE GAME PLAN

You've just lost one job. Why risk becoming a two-time loser?

Before you go to work again, it could be useful to look at some of the reasons why people are fired. If that's what happened to you, you may find out why.

This is a *defensive* game plan, one designed to help keep you from becoming a former employee again.

I realize many people lose jobs for reasons entirely beyond their control. They may be laid off because business is bad. They may be fired not because they are incompetent but because the new boss wants to bring in "his own people." They may be let go because their company is relocating and they can't make the move for one reason or another. They may be out of work because the boss just didn't like their looks.

But let's face it: In many cases, people are fired because they deserve it.

Among the materials I gathered in preparing this book were dozens of responses to a questionnaire I had distributed in the Los Angeles area to people who had lost jobs. Among other things, each was asked what he or she was doing when the bad news came. Donald Imo, who had been working in a dental school, was at home, "having sex with my girlfriend." Lindsay A. Naylor, an aircraft inspector, also was home, "smoking pot." R. Orozco, who identified himself as a "determinations representative," said he was "sleeping on the job." At least he didn't have to wonder why he was fired; but he said he was still "upset."

Herb Marion was working at a gas station, "changing oil in a car," when he got the news. He was "bitter."

"I hit my boss," he said. "I had just got out of jail and wanted to do good. . . . I went back to jail."

Henry Akus, a finance company loan officer, got the news at home while talking with his boss on the phone. "He told me I was not doing the job and making bad loans and losing money for the company," Akus said. "I opened my own business, but I lost it because of gambling. Then I went to work as a fry cook. . . . I just can't get started again."

Arturo Javier, a janitor, was sweeping a floor when the word came. "I threw my broom at my boss," he said. "I went out and bought a paper to look for [another] job. I got a job in a whorehouse that paid more money." He kept telling himself he could "do more than be a janitor." "Now I have started to go to junior college," he said.

Phil Shockie, a brake shop employee, said he was let go during a lunch break one day because there was not enough work to keep him busy. "I collected unemployment," he said. "Then I went into business for myself in my garage and I'm making a lot more money. Getting fired made me get out and hustle."

Howard Buckley, a shipyard worker, told this story: "It was Saturday and a friend of mine called to say we were going to get laid off on Monday. It ruined my weekend." But Buckley seemed to take a philosophical view after that. "I got unemployment for four months," he said. "Then I got rehired when work picked up again. [The layoff] just gave me a vacation. My wife worked, so everything was fine."

Armand Munoz, a barber, said he was on the job when informed he was off the job. "I wanted to kill someone because I was a good barber," he said. "But we didn't have any people coming in. Everyone was letting their hair grow."

That did not mean, however, that Munoz couldn't cut it. He had another job within three months.

For Mark Joseph, a liquor salesman, the axe fell while he was in a bar, drinking. "I didn't care until I sobered up," he said. "Then I asked myself, What am I going to do now?" For a while, he simply kept drinking. "Finally, I joined A.A. and they sobered me up," he said. "I saw that if I didn't get help I'd destroy myself. [So] I went to get help."

Another liquor salesman, Tony Abruzzi, said he was fired because he got a drunk-driving ticket, became uninsurable and could no longer use his car. But there was a happy ending, or at least a happy beginning. "I went to school for another year and got my teaching degree."

Wayne Morrow, a mechanic, also negotiated a satisfying transition. "I was called at home and told not to show up Monday," he said. "I went out and bought a paper and started looking for a job. I got a job in two days, doing a job that had less pressure. A taxi driver. I was never set back because I wanted a job with a lot of free time."

Robert Abramson was a pharmacist. "I was encouraged by my boss to sell prescription tranquilizers to customers even though the prescription did not indicate refill privilege," he said. "My boss implied that I should not call the doctor but to continue the supply to customers. I refused to comply with my boss's unethical demands. He therefore fired me. I felt no remorse.

"I finally found employment as outside representative for a pharmaceutical firm. I recently won a trip to a resort because I was rated as this firm's top salesman."

Carolyn Walker was working in a western clothing store. "I had been discussing the fact that I had asked for several days off far in advance so that I could spend the time with my father up north," she said. "My boss said he was short of staff and, if I went to see my father, not to come back. I left and did not come back.

"I felt deceived, since my boss had made a promise and on that promise I had made plane reservations and had my hopes up for the trip. After visiting my father I found another job and felt no regrets about leaving the previous one. I also felt that if I were in a position of supervisor on a job, I would treat my people fairly and they would be able to depend on my word."

Donald Owings, a financial counselor, said he was fired without ever getting a satisfactory answer as to why. "I felt frustrated," he said, "but also somewhat relieved, since I was not happy with the job and could not identify why.

"I applied immediately for jobs through the employment office, private agencies and in person. I was contacted by a collection agency. . . . They wanted me to obtain the large business firms they had been unable to sell their service to.

"I took the job and obtained the major firms in the city as customers. I was able to manage a coup: They were very pleased when I turned over the account of the major gas company to them. I went from this job to other horizons with great confidence in my abilities."

Most of those who answered the questionnaire were "upset" or "shocked" or "angry" or otherwise disturbed. Leroy Puffer, dropped after a pro football tryout, said, "I wanted to kill someone." Mark Wirth, who had managed a Jack-in-the-Box fast-food outlet, said he threw an egg at the Jack-in-the-Box. Brenda Searcy, a clerk, said she "wanted to cuss them out and tell them to stick it." Bernadette Martinez, a cashier, said of the boss who fired her: "I hate the man." Belinda Lewis, a packer, said her reaction was "the hell with it." Hal Lockwood, a sales representative, said his firing confirmed his belief that most men in business are bastards.

I don't know any of these people. I would not be surprised to learn that some of them were fired unjustly. But it's hard to believe they all were.

Another thing I noticed was that many responded negatively to the question, Did you formulate any game plans? Lockwood asked, "For what game?"

The answer, of course, is for the game coming up when it's time to hunt for another job. But many seemed not to be looking ahead. Carl Banks, an employment representative, was an exception. But he didn't seem to be looking ahead with much focus. Under "Other Comments," he wrote, "There'll always be a brighter day." Let's hope so.

Few said they had expected to be fired. If we assume that at least some of the firings were justified, we may also assume that those fired were doing something wrong without realizing it, or without caring. Unless that changes, their prospects of being fired again are excellent.

Two of the most common reasons why people get fired are nonproductiveness and negative attitude. The first reason, at least, probably does not surprise you. But let's give it a brief look.

Nonproductiveness. The function of business is to make money. This object is achieved by producing goods or services. Every employee is expected to produce his or her share, on time. This law of demand and supply—demand for a given quantity of work to be supplied in a given time—is all but universally enforced. Few employers permit sentiment to get in the way of profit.

You may not produce because you find your job unappealing. But if you don't produce, your boss can hardly be blamed for finding you unappealing. After all, he's probably got somebody looking over his shoulder, too. Maybe another boss. Maybe stockholders. In any event, if you don't produce, your boss is not producing.

Employees may sometimes produce too little because they don't want to extend themselves for "the people with the soft jobs upstairs." They may assume that demands for production decline as jobs get better. This is often a mistaken notion. When a person is promoted from an hourly job to a management position, he has a better job in the sense that he is making more money, and a more enjoyable job in the sense that it's easier to give orders than to take them. His new job also may entail less physical labor. But he gets a new burden: extra responsibilities. That means extra pressure. And he'll most likely work longer hours with no overtime.

There are doubtless many people with jobs no more stimulating than that of the H. Allen Smith character whose function was to count putty knives as they came off an assembly line. I'm not going to insult your intelligence by telling you such a job can be as glamorous as commanding a spaceship, but I do think every job has some importance. As a head coach, I know, I thought that way about the jobs of assistant coaches, equipment managers, trainers, secretaries and even maintenance personnel. Think for a moment and you'll see how much it could hurt a team if these jobs were not properly performed. Start with the bottom people, the maintenance workers. An office simply can't function properly without them. They're indispensable.

When I went to Washington from Los Angeles in 1971, I had to have a secretary. I didn't call a placement agency. I asked Shirley Krystek, my secretary in Los Angeles, to come with me. I knew her. I wanted her experience. It was important.

I'm afraid employers often fail to get this message across to their employees. The boss may understand and appreciate the importance of every procedure in his plant or office, and may assume the employee does, too. It's probably a shaky assumption.

Negative Attitude. Some people love to complain and do it constantly—about the economy, politicians, the weather, the Internal Revenue Service, the local football team, the price of pistachios, their jobs. Especially their jobs. They may just be unhappy people trying to fix blame for their unhappiness on others. Whatever the explanation, they can really make life miserable for those around them. It's as though they think their troubles so singular that everyone should be willing to cancel all engagements to hear about them. They don't seem to recognize a simple truth: People everywhere have problems.

Think about the everyday conversations you had on your last job. If you had a tendency to complain and criticize, work up some new conversational approaches before you get your next job.

Even if you're not a constant critic, one slip can hurt you. A high school teacher told this story:

"As an ex-coach, I was unimpressed with the job done by a varsity coach at our school one year. I thought he lost several games he might have won if he'd prepared the players more thoroughly. I didn't say anything until the start of the following school year, after the coach left for another school. Since he was gone, I saw no harm in it. I told several other teachers and members of the community what a poor job I thought the coach had done. I realize now that it was terribly unprofessional of me. But I thought no more about it until late in the school year, when it was announced that the former coach would be returning to the school—to assume the principal's job. I can remember hoping desperately that the people I'd talked to wouldn't go to the principal and tell him what I'd said. But I knew they would—and they did. It was my own fault. All the trouble could have been avoided if I'd had enough sense to keep my mouth shut."

Complaining can be unproductive, and sometimes counterproductive, not only for employees but for bosses and junior executives. When a supervisor complains to someone about a problem employee, he is almost certainly talking to the wrong person. It's the problem employee, obviously, who should be talked to.

Complaining to third parties presents another risk. If you keep telling X and Y what a lousy job Z is doing, X and Y may stop being open with you, out of fear that you'll start talking about them behind their backs. Also, they may come to view you as a person interested only in talking about problems, not *solving* them. There's an enormous difference.

I used to tell my teams that complaining will rarely move you closer to solutions. It may make you feel better, if your listeners give you a sympathetic ear. And it may make you think you're doing something constructive by pointing out problems. Chances are, however, that you're only fooling yourself into thinking you're accomplishing something.

Arguing can be similarly unproductive. It's excellent mental exercise, but exercising too strenuously can be dangerous. If you argue constantly with coworkers, you can be branded a trouble-maker. If you argue with the boss, he may feel his authority is being challenged. Your arguments may have merit, but you may not have a job. I realize it's frustrating, knowing you're right and having to keep your counsel, but holding your tongue may mean holding your job.

Ours is a sports-minded country, and it has become common to compare companies to athletic teams. You've probably heard business people talking about "game plans" and "ballpark esti-mates" and "carrying the ball" and "touching all the bases" and developing "teamwork" and the like. Some of this terminology is overworked and gets tiresome. But teamwork, for example, really is important in any cooperative undertaking. Whether the goal is to produce quality widgets or successful football seasons, the efforts of many people are necessary to reach the objective. For a group to function effectively, individuals within it must subordinate some of their interests to those of the group as a whole.

You may not be able to bring the same commitment to the Kalabash Can Company that Terry Bradshaw brings to the Pitts-burgh Steelers, but if you work at it you can avoid becoming a negative influence. You may not care about working for the greater glory of Kalabash, but you do care about working. A negative attitude can make you a clog in the machinery instead of a cog. And if you wonder what the people at Kalabash Can Company may do to you then, remember that "Can" is their middle name.

Sometimes workers get into trouble not because of bad atti-tudes but because of "bad vibes" between them and the boss. They run into the sort of personality conflict I had to contend with the first time I worked for the Rams.

Incompatibility can be a real problem, as a secretary once explained: "I didn't like my income, and the boss didn't like my patibility."

That kind of incompatibility is actually a serious matter. But so is the kind that arises when you make a poor first impression on the boss, or have a misunderstanding, or (perhaps quite unintentionally) arouse jealousy of others in your organization.

Incompatibility is not always curable. Sometimes the gears of two personalities simply won't mesh. But sometimes communication helps. If the problem is with your boss, try to talk with him often, without making a nuisance of yourself. Ask for his opinions. Try to fix problems while they're still small and manageable.

But don't be obsequious. Be yourself. Otherwise, you'll have a self-compatibility problem. A high school assistant coach once complained: "We spend so much practice time copying what other teams do that we don't even know what *we* do best." That's one thing that can happen when you try to be somebody else.

One expert offers this advice for dealing with people on a new job: "Be friendly, but not too familiar, during early contact with the new boss. Don't get on a first-name basis unless someone else does, or unless invited to. The best way to get the boss uptight is to suggest making sweeping changes even before you know your job. [Even] if your suggestion is a good one, wait until you've been there a while. . . .

"Avoid anybody who tries to give you a hard time. . . . Among those to watch out for are people who like to gossip and the usual malcontents who . . . put the company down at every opportunity. Stop the gossip-mongers, malcontents, anybody who gives you trouble, by changing the subject as fast as you can. Declare that you are trying to get off on the right foot. . . . Let everyone know you couldn't keep a secret if you had to. . . .

"Company loyalty . . . is one of the strongest supports in favor of your advancing up the ladder. . . . Don't get sidetracked into believing you will get ahead with anything less than a good or superior job performance. . . .

"If you want to gripe, condemn, growl, maybe you should look somewhere else. But until you decide that, and if you want to become a success, let it show in your attitude."[1]

Whether you're new on the job or have been around since the

Roosevelt administration, you're going to make at least an occasional mistake, if not a certifiable blunder. Here's a multiple-
choice test on the best way to handle a situation you've just
mishandled. You should:

    (a) Hope nobody notices.
    (b) Blame it on the guy who quit last week.
    (c) Say you were just checking to see if everybody was alert.
    (d) None of the above.

    The correct answer, of course, is (d). The trouble is it doesn't
tell us what the correct approach is. Perhaps the following ex-
cerpt from a newspaper column will.

    The art of self-promotion has many practitioners, who attribute
their success to varied and often conflicting practices. However, the
way to impress others with your ability may appear quite startling.
Positive information about people, told by themselves, produces a
less favorable impression on others than if told about them by someone else. Perhaps even more significantly, psychologists have found
that *negative information* about people, *told by themselves,* produces
a less negative impression than if from somebody else.[2]

    But how do you go about confessing? And to whom? The same
column recommended these approaches:
    "If the matter is bound to become public knowledge, it's best
for you to 'own up' to it yourself—probably first [to] your boss,
and afterward to other key people who will likely hear of it. A
straightforward explanation is usually best. If there were outside
reasons for the failure or mistake, mention them, but make sure
people know that you accept responsibility for the eventual outcome.
    ". . . It's better to tell more than one person. Thus, several
people will be hearing it directly from you, and the chances of it
sounding even worse than it is will be minimized. Remember,
bad news about yourself sounds least bad coming from you—so
let it reach as many ears as possible."

THE EASY WAY: HARD WORK

Kant Hackett is worried about his job. He has a right to be. He has picked up several early-warning signs that he could wind up before the company firing squad. He dislikes his work, and can't hide it. You can see it in his face. You can hear it when he talks. You can tell it by his indifferent manner. Studies have shown that such manifestations spell short employment expectancy.

Hackett suspects his feelings are becoming known. For one thing, his superiors rarely speak to him now. I used to tell my players, "You don't have anything to worry about as long as I'm talking to you. The time to worry is when I stop talking to you."

When Hackett's supervisors do speak to him, they criticize. The blindfold is about to be slipped into place. Hackett is about to be offered a final cigarette. He has been telling himself for months that he's on the wrong job. And his boss is about to reach the same conclusion.

One cure for Hackett's disease is to make it your goal to be the hardest working employee in the company. How do you go about it? By studying the work habits of hard workers. By concentrating on your work and striving for efficiency, even in seemingly unimportant tasks. By helping others without being asked. By responding positively when asked to assume added responsibility or extra work. By keeping abreast of developments in your field. By not watching the clock. As I suggested earlier, the clock will move as fast as you do. Working hard makes work easier. Taking Hackett's "easy route" only makes it harder.

It could be, of course, that Hackett really is on the wrong job, and should try to make a move before the boss does it for him. But if he has no place to move at the moment, going through the day in slow motion will do him no good. It won't help him now, and it won't help him later when he needs a reference from his present employer.

When I was in high school, I worked in a home nursery one summer as a gardener for a Mr. and Mrs. Couch. I started at thirty cents an hour, working an eight-hour day Monday through Friday. I asked Mr. Couch if I could work ten hours a day. He liked my work. Request granted. Then I asked if I could work weekends as well. Again, he went along. By the end of the summer I was putting in seventy hours a week, and the Couches had let me plant my own garden on their property in an area away from the nursery.

I didn't take the extra work primarily for the money, though thirty cents an hour wasn't bad for a high school kid in those days. I did it because I loved to work.

I haven't changed my outlook since. I'm convinced that success in any endeavor is directly proportional to the amount of work invested in it.

When I took over as head coach of the Rams in 1966, I didn't think we could win on the strength of our personnel alone, even if the players gave what they considered to be 100 percent. So I told them, "One hundred percent is not enough. We must all give 110 percent!" A number of people were kind enough to remind me that it is impossible to give more than 100 percent. But the players knew what I meant. I expected them to give more than they thought they were capable of giving.

And we had a winning season. Eight wins in fourteen games that first year in Los Angeles may not seem like a smashing achievement, but the team was used to losing. The Rams hadn't had a winning season in eight years. The players had to learn how to win—to become conditioned to the idea that only extraordinary effort produces extraordinary teams. It's a gradual process. Such "radical" notions are absorbed slowly. But by the end of my second season in L.A., there were fewer skeptics. Our record that year was 11-1-2.

The fact is most people don't work as hard as they think they do. They imagine they are performing at 90 percent of peak efficiency when they are probably closer to 50 percent. It has not been sufficiently impressed on them that the difference between mediocrity and greatness is extra effort. In an age of mediocre expectations, extra effort offers an extra dividend: Hard workers will stand out even more.

That may sound a bit preachy. But I think it should be said because it's true.

What success I had in coaching was due largely to hard work. In a magazine article some years ago, I wrote: "I have closely studied every coach I have known, head coach and assistant, and I have found very little difference between the best of them and the worst of them. You wonder, Why does this guy win? Why does that guy lose? The guy that loses seems to know his stuff. Yet some are winners and some are losers—both now and probably forevermore. And three things divide them all: total effort versus not quite that much, total preparation versus less than that, and an understanding that winning is living.

"To me the real test of every man and every woman is how much they give of themselves."[3]

The following employee is not someone I know, but you've known employees like him, and so have I. He arrives at the office in the morning at the last minute, or maybe even a few minutes late, complaining that he was tied up in traffic. He wastes fifteen minutes settling down to work. At about 9:45 he starts watching the clock, looking forward to the 10:30 coffee break. At 11:30 he starts watching the clock again, this time looking forward to lunch.

He has the clock under surveillance again soon after lunch, counting down to the mid-afternoon break. If our hero is on a 9-to-5 schedule, he starts watching the clock in earnest about 4 p.m. At 5 he's out the door like a shot. He can't wait to get home, kick off his shoes, collapse in a chair with a drink and tell his wife what a brutal day he had at the office.

In fact, it was a day in which he probably wasted two hours or more. Those who agonize their way through an eight-hour day never work that long, and sometimes not half that long.

I feel sorry for people like that, people who obviously don't enjoy their work. It must be a miserable feeling, going to bed Sunday night dreading Monday morning.

The best way out of such a predicament, of course, is to find a job you can live with. As somebody once put it, "Nothing is really work unless you would rather be doing something else."

Of course, not everyone has the luxury of choosing among a dozen occupations. Many reading this book don't even have a choice of one.

You may be lucky enough to be working but still hate your job. Remember, it's the best one you have. If you can't give it up, you may feel trapped. But there may be a way to improve your situation.

Try to make a name for yourself. If your superiors don't even know your name, you aren't really a person. You're an object, like one of the machines in your office or plant. The best way to make a name for yourself is by attracting attention. By producing.

In every company willing workers are in short supply. Once identified, they may be "overworked," because supervisors would rather impose on them than spin wheels trying to arouse the unwilling. Waste no pity on the victims of this "exploitation." They'll probably be the next generation of supervisors.

A WORD TO THE BOSS

Secretaries and clerks and factory workers aren't the only people who get fired or demoted. It can happen to executives, too. Sometimes, as in the case of ordinary workers, it's not their fault. But sometimes it is.

A friend associated with a large corporation tells a story about a man who did himself out of an executive position. To avoid embarrassing the man further, we'll move him west from his real home base to Hollywood and disguise him as Skyler von Skinn-Flynt, a department head at Reel-Life Films, Incorporated. (In real life, Reel-Life doesn't exist, so far as I know, and I have taken the liberty of inventing situations that parallel those Skyler actually created or confronted. While invented, the situations accurately portray Skyler's problems.)

Skyler had some good qualities. He had joined the department in a secondary capacity and had moved up by working hard and displaying real imagination. He knew what he was doing. And yet, when it came to dealing with people, he didn't know what he was doing. He was not a giving person.

Thinking of Skyler reminds my friend of one of those great Jack Benny radio routines. Benny is accosted by a holdup man and . . .

THIEF: Your money or your life, mister.

Silence.

THIEF: I said your money or your life!

BENNY: I'm thinking! I'm thinking!

In fact, Skyler was close enough with a dollar to make Benny look prodigal. And he was a jealous man. It was a combination that would bring him to grief.

For one thing, Skyler treated the company's money as if it were his own, meaning that anybody who got any of it would know he had been in a fight. People in his department got merit increases and cost-of-living raises. Skyler couldn't help that; it was company policy. The problem was that he demanded far more for the money than Reel-Life Films ever would have wanted—or would have tolerated had it known what he was up to.

The company filmed television commercials. Naturally, most of the work was done in the field. Skyler couldn't stand the thought that some of his people might be putting in short hours. If they were working in town, on a job starting later than 10 a.m., they had to report to the office when it opened at 9, though no useful purpose was served by this procedure. There was nothing for them to do in the office before leaving.

Skyler's directors and camera crews were on salary. If they got ahead of schedule, finishing a job at, say, 2:30 p.m. instead of 5 p.m., they were expected to report back to the office and stay there until 5, though there was nothing they could accomplish there.

Skyler managed to alienate practically everyone who worked for him. His demands were plainly irrational, and his people saw right through them, correctly concluding that Skyler was motivated by meanness. So far as the company was concerned, all that really mattered was the quality of work produced. Reel-Life's management had not the slightest interest in whether a camera crew knocked off at noon or midnight, so long as the job was done properly and the production schedule was met. But Skyler had a crabbed view of life. He was always afraid somebody would "get away with something," that somebody would not be working when he was. In fact, it almost seemed to bother him that other people might be having a good time.

That ties in with another of his unfortunate qualities: He was selfish. If a trip had to be taken to Death Valley to work with a sponsor's people on a commercial in mid-August (when a cold snap might bring the temperature down to 110 degrees), Skyler would dispatch an assistant. But if a trip had to be made to set up a commercial in Hawaii or Paris or Bermuda, Skyler would announce that this was a matter requiring the personal attention of the department head. He routinely grabbed off all the good trips, though the work they entailed could have been handled by any of his assistants. Some might view this as a proper exercise of executive privilege. Skyler's subordinates were not inclined to that view. They saw him as a man interested only in himself. Whatever privileges his rank gave him, he was undermining the department's morale and hurting his company.

His jealousy inflicted further damage. Skyler was tormented by the knowledge that he made considerably less money than some of the actors and actresses who appeared in Reel-Life commercials. He said it wasn't fair. "These prima donnas do a thirty-second spot every two months," he was fond of saying, "and live in Beverly Hills." He was obsessed by what he perceived to be a monstrous injustice, of which he was the principal victim. "These people do nothing for society," he would say. "They don't deserve to get rich hawking dog biscuits and deodorant. Sure, we make money out of it, too. But we're the ones doing the real work. These phony actors just stand there, reading somebody else's material, and get paid like they were doing *Gone With the Wind*. They make me sick!"

The people around Skyler could have tolerated this monologue had it been an occasional thing. But he gave regular performances, sometimes doing replays to make sure no one missed the point. This wore on his subordinates, who of course did not feel free to walk out in the middle of a performance. But it did more than that. It persuaded them they were working for a man with serious problems.

Presently Skyler's unpopularity was not only well established in his own department but well known throughout the company. Luckily for him, the people in the executive suite were not trigger-happy. A firing or demotion was a rare event at Reel-Life. And, in truth, Skyler's department was performing satisfactorily, though its productiveness was certainly due more to the professionalism of the staff than to inspirational leadership.

While Skyler was in no immediate danger, his superiors were naturally somewhat concerned about morale in his department. And Skyler would soon make a troubling situation worse.

One of the companies for which Reel-Life regularly did commercials was a major automaker, Belchfire Motors. Over the years a cordial relationship had developed between Reel-Life and Belchfire. At a dinner on location one night, a Belchfire executive offered to supply cars to Reel-Life at well below fleet prices. "Just tell us how many you want," the Belchfire executive said.

Skyler was assigned to put in the order. He ordered one car extra, for himself.

Belchfire mailed papers confirming the order. But they got misrouted. Instead of going to Skyler, they wound up in Reel-Life's main offices. An executive there remembered Skyler had told him five cars would be ordered. But the papers showed six. Questions were asked. Skyler didn't have the right answers.

He had not tried to steal anything. He was going to buy the car (paying thousands below list price). But he had put Reel-Life in an awkward position. The understanding had been that Belchfire would supply cars for Reel-Life's use on company business, not for the personal use of company employees. There was a difference. A client's generosity had been abused.

And so had the patience of Reel-Life's management.

Skyler was relieved as head of his department and given a subordinate position in the same department. It was his turn to be in an awkward position. He was now just a soldier in a platoon he had once commanded.

Lesson: A boss who demands much of others must demand much of himself. If he constantly preaches against the evils of cutting corners while cutting a few himself, his employees will catch on to his hypocrisy. And he will then be working in a nest of enemies.

A boss doesn't have to be permissive to be liked. In fact, an undemanding boss is apt to be perceived as weak. And a demanding boss may develop a fiercely loyal following. Vince Lombardi, the great Green Bay coach, drove his players relentlessly. (You may remember the great line attributed to defensive tackle Henry Jordan: "He treats us all the same—like dogs.") But few coaches have been more highly regarded by their players. Lombardi showed his team that his discipline had a purpose. He was teaching a subject called winning, and his class was graduated with honors.

In the end, much depends on the spirit a boss brings to his job. If he asks a lot, but gives a lot, he'll probably get a lot. But if he comes to the job with a mean spirit, ordering people around for no other purpose than to flaunt his power, he will soon have aroused more resentment than respect. And, eventually, he will probably be defeated, by himself.

A boss should also be careful about how he goes about building his empire. Nearly all bosses have at least a little empire builder in them, and it's not necessarily a bad quality. Building a bigger company, or a bigger department, can mean doing bigger things —and producing more jobs. But while some empire builders have made life better for their communities, others have made it plain miserable for all around them.

"The point where ambition becomes overzealousness is difficult to define precisely," said a story in a computer industry magazine. "However, a relevant warning signal is when the forces that drive a person forward start turning against the best interests of the company. . . . Mayford Roark [executive director of systems at Ford Motor Company] distinguishes between 'people who are ambitious' and 'the guy who reeks of it.' Those who are desirably ambitious, he says, 'have a certain amount of faith in the organization which leads them to believe that what is good for the company is good for them, too. The guy who is over-ambitious is opportunistically maneuvering for short-term advantage, and hurting colleagues in the process.'

" 'There's nothing wrong with ambition, but you have to maintain a perspective on it,' suggests Donald D. Buchanan, executive vice president of the North Carolina National Bank in Charlotte. 'If you're ambitious beyond your capabilities, you're bound to drown.' "[4]

You're doubtless familiar with the term "quality control." If empire building is one of your qualities, learn to control it.

SOME ADVICE ABOUT ADVICE

I can't very well promise you a proven formula for avoiding the axe if you're a boss because I'm an ex-boss four times over. But I think I did some things right, and I think I observed other bosses doing things wrong. Some of them may have been fired because their bosses observed the same mistakes I did.

One sure way for a person in a supervisory position to get himself into trouble is to take advice from others without checking it out. Getting advice in a way is like getting a new player. One of the first things you do is weigh it.

I've found this particularly true when it comes to asking about people you're thinking of hiring. In the National Football League, I knew people who raved about everyone. You'd be thinking about hiring an assistant coach or a front-office person and you'd ask for evaluations from general managers and head coaches on teams the person had been associated with. "Excellent," they'd say. "Really excellent."

Everybody was at least excellent. Some were rated higher.

The people who offered these evaluations may have thought

they were doing a favor for the person being evaluated. But I soon discovered they were doing no favors for me. If everybody was "excellent," how come some of those people they recommended had been let go by six clubs in the face of their excellence?

I once put a sign on my desk, facing me. It said, "Evaluate the Evaluator."

I began to learn the lesson when I was with the Chicago Bears, before I went to Los Angeles. One of my job titles at Chicago was personnel director. In that capacity I had to get player evaluations from college coaches all over the country. It was amazing how some coaches would oversell their players. I began to think I was dealing with a bunch of closet used-car salesmen.

Naturally, we had our own scouts evaluate all prospects. If we hadn't, we wouldn't have been able to recognize some of our rookies when they got to training camp. They'd turn up two inches shorter and twenty-five pounds lighter than their college coaches had advertised. Players we were told could do forty yards in 4.5 seconds would come closer to 5.4. I half-expected some college coach to send me a note saying, "This kid has exceptional peripheral vision—from both heads. If you can spare the extra helmet, you'll have yourself a real blue-chipper here. He's truly extraordinary under pressure. If he loses his head, he's still got one left over."

On the other hand, there are people who go off in the opposite direction. Hampton Pool, once an NFL coach and now a top scout, is one of them. Hamp never goes overboard. Sometimes, in fact, he goes a little underboard. He rates players rigidly, and his reports tend to emphasize negative points. So you have to make a sort of reverse allowance in the player's favor.

Personally, I'd rather get reports from a scout like Hamp Pool. At least when his players show up, you're never disappointed.

One reason you can come by a lot of bum information in professional football is that some of the club executives and coaches are hired by owners whose knowledge of the game is considerably less comprehensive than they think. The executives and coaches may have been recommended to the owner by people whose football knowledge is similarly limited. This produces some interesting results.

A team fails on the field. We may not know for sure whose fault it is. But we know who's going to get fired. The coach.

So the general manager hires a new coach. This often solves nothing. One reason could be that coaching was not really the problem. The problem could have been higher up, with the people who almost never get fired. If you're a football fan you can probably think of teams that have had four coaches in six years —and six losing seasons in six years. Either coaching was not the problem or the club leadership was incapable of selecting a coach who could solve the problem.

Not that the owner has to worry about going broke because he is surrounded by incompetents and may be one himself. With the millions each franchise gets from television every year, Mortimer Snerd couldn't bankrupt an NFL franchise. Everybody profits but the fans.

Don't misunderstand. I'm not talking about all NFL clubs. Some are run by first-rate football folk, really bright people. But many are not. By the standings you shall know them.

There's a saying that describes their predicament. It's sort of a triple negative, but I think you'll catch the drift: "They don't know—but they don't know they don't know."

Sportswriter Tom Boswell touched on the point in an engaging essay on the perils of coaching in contemporary professional football. He quoted a number of coaches and ex-coaches, including me. Samples:

Chuck Knox, Buffalo Bills: "The last time I saw a figure, the average tenure of an NFL coach was 2.4 years. We make a running back's life expectancy look great by comparison. . . . Unfortunately, it takes unusually smart ownership to resist all the pressures to change coaches every time there's a problem. They know the devil they've got, but they forget to think about the devil they're going to bring in next. Buffalo is a perfect example. For twenty years they had the worst record in the NFL.

. . . The reason is the constant changes of head coaches. They kept the [executives] who were supplying the bad talent, but fired the poor guys who got stuck with it."

Hank Stram, former coach of the Kansas City Chiefs and New Orleans Saints: "We're in the era of the Charlie McCarthy coach. You're the dummy and somebody else pulls the strings. Vince Lombardi couldn't make it now. Some accountant would get the owner's ear and undermine him. The third man—the guy between you and the owner—is the franchise ruiner. The story's always the same. Just change the names from Stram to Allen to Bum Phillips to Jack Pardee."

Tom Landry, Dallas Cowboys: "Hank said that? Well, is that any different than the rest of corporate America? It's executive-level politics. Our new NFL owners didn't grow up with the game like the old families—the Halases and Rooneys—so they frequently need advice. And, you know, the sources of that advice are sometimes unreliable. . . . I don't like the trend. I see too many old friends and good coaches who are out of work without sufficient reason. . . .

"Football is still primarily emotion. Hitting comes first. Thinking comes second. So my job is to get men to do what they don't want to do—punish themselves. If you give them an out, a way to avoid the pain and not pay the price, they'll take it. Not consciously. But subconsciously. They'll take the 'out.'

"How do you get them to pay that price in punishment to themselves? Well, one of the best ways is to make sure that they are concerned about keeping their jobs. And they won't be if they think that the coach may not keep his job."

Bud Grant, Minnesota Vikings: "People like Stram and Allen can't get back in the game because they're too strong. As coaches, we have no union, no bargaining agent, no protection and no strength to deal from.

"We are purposely kept in that position by the league. We are resented because we have so much impact on the game. Pro football is a coach's medium and always has been. So the league sees us as a necessary evil. We're muzzled. . . .

"Everything you say is supposed to be 'positive.' . . . If I'd known twenty-five years ago what I know now, I don't know if I'd have gotten into this profession."

George Allen: "NFL coaches are getting to be like those Datsun cars. You can't tell 'em apart.

"Why don't I have a head-coaching job? 'Cause they're afraid of me. If you're not a puppet, you're in trouble."[5]

Unless all these people are wrong, there is some misguided management in professional football. Now it may be that there is less bad advice in general circulation than in the NFL. But didn't somebody tell Chrysler a few years ago to stick with big cars? Maybe it was the same guy who told Ford the Edsel couldn't miss. Or perhaps a descendant of the guy who told Columbus he couldn't possibly sail "around" the world because, as any fool could plainly see, the earth was flat as a pizza.

If you've got a problem and you can't find a solution, you obviously need advice. But, again, watch out where you get it.

General rule: Before following anyone's advice, know his credentials. It's not enough that he's highly intelligent, a straight shooter and a nice guy. He must have a solid track record in the area about which you want advice.

Exception to general rule: Sometimes the soundness of advice is self-evident, and it doesn't matter who the source is. You may have heard the story about the college professor who had a flat tire and stopped on a street running alongside the grounds of an insane asylum. The professor jacked up his car, removed the hub cap from the wheel with the flat and took off the lug nuts. He placed the hub cap face down, using it as a bowl to store the lug nuts in while he got his spare tire. But when he stood up to get the spare, he accidentally kicked the hub cap and all the nuts fell through an iron grating in the gutter and into the municipal sewer system.

The professor sat on the curb to ponder his predicament. After five minutes, he had thought of nothing but a string of high-brow obscenities. Then a voice behind him said, "Psst! Hey, mister." The voice belonged to a man standing inside the fence surrounding the mental hospital. He was obviously a resident of the facility. He had been watching the professor's roadside adventure from the start.

"Hey, mister," the man repeated. "Why don't you take one nut off each of the other wheels? That'll give you three nuts to hold your spare wheel on till you can get to a service station."

The professor was much obliged—and much embarrassed.

"Suffering Cicero!" he said. "Why wasn't I smart enough to think of that?"

Before leaving the subject of advice, let's look at the flip side. Whether you're an executive or just one of the troops, it's as important to be careful when giving advice as when taking it. You can only hurt yourself by offering suggestions merely because you've been asked for them and are afraid to say, "I don't know."

Similarly, you should be careful about recommending people for jobs. Don't give anyone a glowing recommendation just because he is a friend. This could hurt both of you. If the friend is not equipped for the job, you're doing him no favor by helping him get it. You may just be setting him up for a dismissal. And if you keep recommending people who are ill equipped, the word will get around and your reputation will suffer.

On the other hand, if a friend asks you to put in a good word with a prospective employer, and you know the friend can handle the job, don't hesitate to give him a nice buildup. In fact, go out of your way to help him. If he gets the job and performs well, you'll both benefit. His success will be recognized and you'll be remembered as one of the people who could see his potential.

I was happy one time to be able to put in a good word for Roman Gabriel, who had played quarterback for me in Los Angeles and won the NFL's most-valuable-player award one season. Roman wanted the head coaching job at Cal Poly Pomona and asked if I'd recommend him. I called the athletic director's office. His secretary said he was busy. He had been swamped with calls, was interviewing someone at the moment and had someone else waiting for an interview. I left my name and number.

Two days passed. My call hadn't been returned. I knew Roman had a lot of competition for the job and didn't have much coaching experience to offer. If I was going to help him, I'd better get with it. So I called the athletic director's office again. This time I got through.

"You're fortunate Roman Gabriel is interested in the job," I said. "Frankly, I'm surprised that he is. But he can do a lot for your athletic program just by his presence."

The director thanked me for the call. He apologized for not having gotten back to me. He was new on the job and had really been snowed under. I told him not to hesitate to call me again if he needed any more of my thoughts on Gabriel.

He phoned about a week later and said Roman was one of three finalists. If I were doing the hiring, I said, I'd immediately trim the field of finalists to one. "Your program needs someone like Roman," I said.

I'm not sure how much weight my recommendation carried, but Roman got the job. I didn't lobby for him in the expectation that he could turn his team into another Alabama or Michigan (that's not what football is about at a college like Cal Poly), but I was confident he could produce a program in which he and the school could take pride.

I was even more aggressive in my support of Marv Levy when he was trying to get the head coaching job with the Kansas City Chiefs. Marv at the time was coaching the Montreal Alouettes in the Canadian Football League. He had formerly been one of my assistant coaches. The Chiefs called me several times and I called them once, without being asked, to recommend Levy. In one conversation I asked John Steadman, the club president, how he was coming along with his interviewing. He said they had more people to talk to and no one had an edge at the moment.

"Well," I said, "I'll tell you one thing: If Marv Levy isn't either number one or two on your list, the people conducting this task should be fired." I was talking, of course, about John himself. But that was how I felt. I wanted to help Lamar Hunt, the club owner, and I wanted to help Marv. I think it's worth selling hard when you really believe in a person.

But, again, make sure you know what you're selling. Making a few bad recommendations may not cost you your own job, but negatives add up. Whether you're an executive or a spear carrier, you want to avoid them. It makes for greater occupational longevity.

HANDLING PEOPLE

So does knowing how to deal with people. This, of course, is a subject that would make for an entire book—and has, for authors like Robert M. Bramson, a management consultant who wrote *Coping With Difficult People* (Anchor Press/Doubleday). Bramson also has lectured on the subject, and I recently read a newspaper story about one of his talks:

"There are the Sherman tanks. The complainers. The superagreeables. The negativists. The know-it-all experts. The snipers. The indecisive stallers. The silent clams. And, most dramatic of all, the exploders.

"Bob Bramson contends most difficult people fit into one or more of those character types and, while you might not want to spend a lot of time with them, he's found some techniques to make life more productive when you have to."[6]

"Sherman tanks," we learn from Bramson, "have strong needs to prove to themselves and others that their view of the world is always right. They feel righteous anger toward those who do not do as they 'should,' which justifies hurting them. They expect others to run from them, and [they] devalue them when they do."

When you see a Sherman tank coming, you're supposed to avoid direct combat. It's not easy to get the best of a tank, and even if you do, you may be in trouble, because shot-up Sherman tanks are likely to turn into snipers.

The trick is to stand up to Sherman tanks without trying to defeat them. If they become intimidating, and they will, say you don't agree with them. But remember you're only trying to stand up to them, not knock them down. Don't try to draw them into an argument from which they will emerge devastated. Just show them you're strong, and they'll probably respect you.

Snipers, as their name suggests, are less heavily armed than Sherman tanks. They don't run over you. Instead, they pin you down with verbal small-arms fire. They don't come out in the open. They make critical remarks from camouflage, not identifying you by name as the target but clearly intending to hit you.

Bramson suggests trying to draw them out in the open, perhaps by saying, "That sounded like a dig. Did you mean it that way?" If the answer is yes, it is appropriate to express displeasure. This may discourage further attacks.

Exploders are adults who throw childish tantrums, often defensively when things are falling apart for them. Bramson's suggestion: "Give them time to run down and regain self-control on their own. If they don't, break into their tantrum state by saying or shouting a neutral phrase such as 'Stop!' Show that you take them seriously. And if needed and possible, get a breather and get some privacy with them."

The *indecisive staller* may be afraid any decision he makes will hurt somebody. So he doesn't make one. A decision may sometimes be drawn out of him by engaging him in conversation and getting him to talk about specific reservations standing in the way of a decision. This can expose the real issues. You can then examine them with the staller and perhaps lead him to the decision you want by describing the beneficial results of adopting such a decision.

Clams, of course, are people who won't talk. "Clams learned to shut up when the going was tough precisely because someone else always rescued them by talking," Bramson says. One way to handle them is bluntly: "I thought we were going to have a conversation. You're not saying anything." Or, if something is to be decided, you might say that the clam's silence means you'll just have to make the decision yourself.

The *know-it-all* requires no definition. One way to deal with him is by asking questions about his opinions (of which there will of course be many) rather than challenging the opinions head-on.

If you ask enough questions, he may come to view you as an equal—in other words, as a fellow know-it-all.

A *complainer* may respond positively to people who listen to him attentively and then ask exactly how he'd like things to be. Confronted with this question, Bramson says, the complainer "may find himself or herself dealing with the situation in a problem-solving way." If you don't give the complainer any satisfaction, you may still get something for your effort. The complainer may give up on you, Bramson says, "and go away and find someone else more satisfying to complain to."

Negativists are graduate complainers. They have a wet-blanket quality and their motto is, "It can't be done." Don't try to persuade them they're wrong by arguing directly against their position. Instead, try to offset their negativism by making realistically optimistic statements. You have to watch out for negativists, Bramson says. "A good negativist can get a whole group of people demotivated to solve a problem."

Superagreeables always say things that are nice to hear. To make you feel good, they'll tell you anything. This may produce superdisagreeable results. For example, a superagreeable may tell you he's anxious to tackle a project and can complete it by next Tuesday. It will be impossible to complete it by then, but he doesn't want to tell you that. It would violate the code of superagreeableness.

Bramson's prescription for dealing with superagreeables: "Make honesty nonthreatening. Many times all that's needed is a straightforward request for an honest opinion, especially when it can be sincerely accompanied by words that say, 'I really want to know what's on your mind because I value your friendship.' Don't allow superagreeables to make unrealistic commitments. Be prepared to compromise in order to resolve the problem to your ultimate best advantage. Since superagreeables tend to be most apprehensive in situations in which they are likely to lose the favor of others, they are partial to win-win solutions."

This is just a brief introduction to some of the character types that everyone—boss and employee—has to deal with on the job. The better you can deal with them, the better off you'll be on your present job or your next one. I'd recommend reading Bramson's *Coping With Difficult People* and other books in the field. For the employee, knowing how to handle fellow workers may make life on the job easier. For the boss, knowing how to handle workers is essential to survival. An extended study of the problem would be beyond the scope of this book, but I'd like to touch on a point or two that every aspiring boss should know and that many disemployed bosses should understand to avoid getting fired again.

Any time you promote or give special recognition to an employee, you've got a potential problem on your hands. Those not promoted or recognized may resent what you've done.

I went through this many times as a general manager charged with making decisions affecting not only players but coaches, trainers, equipment men, team doctors and front-office personnel. There is not always a simple solution. If a player is not doing his job, you may be able to correct or alleviate the problem by moving him to another position. You may move a guard to tackle, for example, or a center to another interior-line position. But it's probably harder to "find another department" for a football player than for an office worker. That's why general managers and coaches do a lot more firing proportionately than most other bosses. (Whenever a player is cut from a team, he is fired, in effect if not in fact.)

Football executives, no doubt like executives in other fields, are caught between personal feelings and professional responsibility when trying to decide whether to keep an employee or let him go. Suppose, for example, that you have used a high draft choice to acquire a player or have traded for him. And suppose that player has not performed as expected. Emotion is apt to point you one way and logic another. You've got pride invested in the situation because it was your choice to get the player in the first place. Letting him go is admitting you're wrong. And that, of course, is an admission most of us make only reluctantly.

You may find yourself making excuses for the player. He's a rookie and hasn't had time to acclimate himself to the professional game. Or he came from another team and is trying to learn a foreign system. You may be right. Or you may just be trying to justify your acquisition of the player.

The rule I tried to follow when considering a player move was to ask myself, Will it make us a stronger team? Will it help us win? If the answer was a confident yes, I knew I had to make the move no matter whose feelings were hurt. Sometimes they were my own.

A common mistake is to keep someone around, and maybe even advance him, because he has a pleasant smile and makes a nice appearance. When you do this you may be overreacting to a favorable quality and assuming the person must have other qualities, as yet undemonstrated. My experience teaches that this is a dangerous assumption.

It's not easy to overcome your emotions when you're considering a decision that will hurt someone you've taken a liking to. It's hard to let a player go, particularly when you've not only played the part of hirer and firer but have also appeared in the role of firee. It's a fact of life, though, that not everyone can stay on the roster when a football team cuts down—any more than every probationary employee can survive in conventional business. The important thing is that the decision be based on reason, not emotion. I tried to stick by that rule and would like to think it generally made more sense when I fired somebody than when somebody fired me.

1. Carl F. Denny, Carlden Personnel Service, "On the Job Front," *New York Post*, September 2, 1980.
2. Auren Uris and Jane Bensahel, "On the Job: Let Others Tell of Your Greatness," *Los Angeles Times*, April 13, 1981. [Italics added.]
3. George Allen, with Joe Marshall, "A Hundred Percent Is Not Enough," *Sports Illustrated*, July 9, 1973.
4. Martin Lasden, "Avoid the Empire-Building Image," *Computer Decisions*, October 1981.
5. Thomas Boswell, *Washington Post*, "In the NFL, the Best Way to Avoid a Sack Is Stay Low-Key," *Los Angeles Times*, February 4, 1981.
6. Beth Ann Krier, "Handling Difficult People," *Los Angeles Times*, July 14, 1981.

7 / *For Sale: You*

THE RESUME

Losing a job paradoxically leaves you with a full-time job: looking for another one. In many cases, one of the most important aspects of this search will be summed up in a few words. You will write those words, then rewrite them, then maybe rewrite the rewritten version. The finished product will be your resume.

Not everyone needs a resume. One ordinarily is not expected, for example, from a job-seeking auto mechanic, bricklayer, pipefitter—or professional football coach.

In most professional fields, however, a resume is not only useful but indispensable. A worksheet prepared by Bernard Haldane Associates, a Boston-based job counseling firm, puts it this way:

"Your resume is a . . . dynamic and factual representation of you at your best. It is also an indication of future achievement. An employer can only hire your future. A resume has three purposes:

"1—To present your job and career objective in terms of your greatest strengths and . . . in a positive and unique way.

139

"2—To prove that your job and career objective is realistic, and supported by related experience and accomplishments.

"3—To enable you to take control of interviews by using your resume as a 'script' and as a point of reference."

Whole books have been written about the art of preparing resumes. In one, Marian Faux writes:

"Resumes are the hallmark of the capable, professional worker. They show off your intelligence, your organizational and thinking skills, and your ability to sell yourself.

"A resume is first of all a selling tool. Its purpose is to sell you. The preparation of a resume, therefore, is no light matter. It requires days of thought, preparation and actual writing."[1]

And yet it may run no more than a single typewritten page. In fact, that may be a good length to shoot for. A resume of more than two pages is probably in need of tightening. Keep in mind that the person who reads your resume may have to read dozens or even hundreds more in a week. You are probably most apt to "grab" that reader with a terse, meticulously organized resume. He or she doesn't want the unabridged story of your life.

It may be a good idea to prepare your resume in several stages. In the original draft, you should not be preoccupied with length. In summary form, write down everything of possible use. You can cut and refine later.

A common heading is one that informs the reader at once what he or she is reading and who you are. Example:

Resume of
Alan George
1008 Greystone Avenue
Fireman's Gap, New Mexico 87565
Phone: (505) 001-1001

Getting that out of the way at the beginning avoids any possibility of falling into one blunder you'd think would never be committed but occasionally is, as Marian Faux relates:

"The personnel director of a Fortune 500 company reported

his frustration at receiving the perfect resume from what appeared to be the perfectly qualified candidate for a very high position—only to discover that it contained no name or address."

The first section under the name and address may be one headed "Job Objective." It may combine a statement of your objective with a background summary. Example:

Objective: Executive position in personnel training and development. Experience includes 12 years in personnel training, consulting, sales and marketing.

Other sections of the resume may be used to summarize your employment history, job accomplishments, education, military service, language proficiencies, professional memberships, authorship of articles or books and any personal information you may wish to include. Be concise. It's all right—even desirable most of the time—to omit the first-person pronoun. For instance:

Related
Accomplishments:

Saved $55,000 annually in salaries of new personnel by training initially reluctant department heads in modern employee-development methods. Program now in third year.

Persuaded management to triple size of employee-development program by demonstrating its direct contribution to company profits, with minimum investment, using present staff.

Remember, the resume is supposed to be a summary of *relevant* information. If you're looking for a job with a bank, never mind your affiliation with the Baroque Music Society. The bank is interested in notes, but not the kind Bach wrote.

Avoid volunteering extensive personal information. If you think giving your age might hurt you, omit it. If you're over forty, for example, saying so could cost you an interview. Your age will be more or less apparent, of course, if you get the interview. But at least then you'll have a chance to persuade the interviewer that you have enough to offer to overcome whatever handicap your age presents. In her *Resume Guide,* Marian Faux offers this advice: "A good rule of thumb is to include the bare minimum of personal information that will be required for you to obtain an interview. If you are comfortable including personal information, the most you will probably want to include is your birthdate (not your age, which changes every year), marital status, willingness to relocate and willingness to travel."

Watch your spelling and grammar. Double check for errors. Then recheck. "It definitely pays to have another pair of eyes take a look," Faux says. "One woman who was applying for the position of bank vice president let her nine-year-old daughter take a look at the last draft of her resume and was both delighted and dismayed when the child spotted a grammatical error."

Spelling and grammatical errors were among ten common resume mistakes identified by another author, Tom Jackson. He reported that surveys of employers, job counselors and employment agencies showed resumes were most often criticized because they were:

1—*Too long.* One side of one page is the generally preferred length.

2—*Disorganized.* Information is hard to follow if scattered. It must be grouped logically.

3—*Poorly typed.* Resumes must have a professional look.

4—*Overwritten.* Individual sections run on, taking "too long to say too little."

5—*Too sparse.* Some things, like job titles, can't be omitted. A resume can be too long overall and still too sparse in some vital respects. If you're aiming for a one-page resume and you produce a draft that runs a page and one quarter, don't assume you've included everything necessary just because you've exceeded your target length. Make sure you've covered *all* essentials, then look for nonessential information to trim.

6—*Not oriented for results.* Resumes must show what their authors have accomplished. The assumption otherwise will be that they have accomplished nothing.

7—*Weakened by too many irrelevancies.* For resume purposes, height, weight and sex are not vital statistics.

8—*Not carefully proofread.* Letting a prospective employer find misspellings and grammatical errors in your resume is giving him a good excuse for not even talking to you.

9—*Too pretentious.* "Fancy typesetting and binders, photographs and exotic paper stocks distract from the . . . presentation."

10—*Misdirected.* Too many resumes are circulated at random. If sent to a company unrequested, the resume should be accompanied by a cover letter explaining what position the applicant seeks.[2]

One of my neighbors, John Whelan, a retired educator, tells me there is only one inflexible rule in resume writing: Be honest.

"You should never undersell your abilities, training or experience," he says. "But the surest way to kill any interest a personnel manager may have in you is to make exaggerated claims that cannot be verified. People who hire have been subjected to so many inaccurate claims in fancy packages that they look on resumes with a very critical eye.

"A resume, though, is still the basic tool in job seeking. It is the key which will open the door to the interview that will secure the job. It is also of great importance in making you aware of your own abilities and ambitions. All resumes follow a pretty standard form. You can decide for yourself what specific variations will be most effective in helping you catch the attention of the person who will give you a job."

While it is true, as Whelan suggests, that resume forms are quite standard, there are at least several ways of presenting the standardized information. Probably the most familiar format is that of the chronological resume. Under "Employment History," jobs held by the applicant are listed in chronological order, beginning with the most recent and working back. The same pattern is followed in a section commonly headed "Education."

One alternative to the chronological resume is the functional resume. Writer Tom Jackson, quoted earlier in this section, describes the difference:

"While the chronological resume emphasizes work experience and personal history, the functional variety puts the stress on the individual's basic ability and potential. This form allows the writer to organize and highlight information toward a particular career target."

In the functional resume, important job accomplishments may be listed high up without identifying employers or giving dates of employment. This permits the applicant to reach back a job or two and give high billing to achievements that may have particular application to the job now being sought.

Suppose, for example, that a female executive wishes to mention three job achievements but that the one most relevant to the position she seeks was accomplished on her second-to-last job. In a chronological resume, she would have to mention her most recent job first. In a functional resume, she may mention the second-to-last job first, to make sure it catches the prospective employer's eye.

Later, near the end of the resume, she will give a brief history, listing jobs and employers in chronological order. Essentially, she has supplied the same information she would have in a chronological resume. She has simply shifted the emphasis. If the resume lands her an interview, she must of course be prepared to identify her most relevant achievement with a particular job and to explain why she listed that achievement out of order. Her answer will be the truth: She wanted to lead off with her strongest legitimate credential. (This assumes, of course, that she did not reach back ten or twenty years for her first-mentioned accomplishment. That would be an ill-advised deception.)

In his article on resume formats, Tom Jackson writes that the functional format may be most effective for people who "want to emphasize capabilities not used in recent work experience" or who are re-entering the job market after an appreciable absence or who have held a number of relatively unconnected jobs. The functional resume is not the best way to go, he says, for those who "want to emphasize a management growth pattern" or whose most recent employer is "highly prestigious" or who are in "highly traditional fields such as teaching, ministerial [and] political, where the specific employers are of paramount importance."

If you have more than one skill, you may be sending resumes to companies in different fields or in discrete parts of one field. In this case, you should probably write two or more resumes, each aimed at a particular target. The points you emphasize in a resume for Company X may not be the ones Company Y would find most impressive. This does not mean you have to start a second resume from scratch. A little shift of emphasis will often be sufficient.

Several sample resumes appear on the following pages and may be used as models. If you'd like more examples, you can find books on the subject at public libraries. If you want professional help, try "Resume Service" in the Yellow Pages of your telephone directory.

Roberta Wells
1300 Wilson Avenue
St. Louis, Missouri 63119
Phone: (314) 487-4855

Job Objective

Position as designer of women's apparel

Employment History

Junior House Designs, Ltd., 1976–1979

Trainee. Worked as a sample maker, pattern maker, cutter and machine operator.

Assistant product manager. Responsibilities included estimating production costs, scheduling work flow, hiring and training new workers, controlling quality, supervising overall production activities, some bookkeeping.

Education

Rhode Island School of Design, 1972–1976

Scholarship student
Awarded Golden Ace Student Design Award
Design, major; business administration, minor

Personal

Married, with one child
Will relocate; will travel

References and samples available on request.

Marian Faux, *The Complete Resume Guide* (New York: Monarch Press, 1980).

RESUME OF MARILYN MANSFIELD

50 Eureka Blvd.
Oshkosh, Wisconsin 99901
Phone (331) 313-3130

Job Objective	Director of marketing leading to general manager within three years.
Education 1972–1974	UNIVERSITY OF PENNSYLVANIA, PHILADELPHIA PA. M.B.A., June 1974

FOR SALE: YOU / 147

1970–1972	COLUMBIA UNIVERSITY, NEW YORK, N.Y. B.S., Chemical Engineering, June 1972.
1966–1970	UNIVERSITY OF IDAHO, MOSCOW, ID. B.A., Chemistry, June 1970

Business Experience December 1978– Present	CONSOLIDATED SOAP, SAN FRANCISCO, CA. Brand manager for marketing and P & L responsibility for company's second largest brand. Turned business around through marketing and product improvements.
June 1978– December 1978	BEATRICE FOODS CO., CHICAGO, ILL. Brand Manager for La Choy. Complete marketing responsibility for $30M brand.
April 1976– June 1978	Assistant Brand Manager, AUNT NELLIE'S FOODS. Executed successful restaging.
November 1975–April 1976	Sales Representative. Sold all frozen entree brands.
August 1974– November 1975	Brand Assistant, TROPICANA JUICES. Planned and executed complete national restaging.
Summer, 1973	BOISE CASCADE CORP., CASCADE ENVELOPE DIV., ADDISON, ILL. Group captain for 10 paper converting lines and 55 employees.

Summers, 1966–1972	BOISE CASCADE CORP., BOISE, IDAHO. Chemical Engineer. Process engineering.
Personal Background	Grew up in Oregon, Utah and Wisconsin. Activities include travel, photography, entomology.

Tom Ballantyne, "Getting a Job: Reading Between the Lines," *National Business Employment Weekly,* August 9, 1981. [Resume reproduced in slightly altered form.]

RESUME

Walter J. Ward
9001 W. Vermont Avenue
Los Angeles, CA 90028
(213) 009-6900

DESIRED

Sales managerial position.

QUALIFICATIONS

Six years of experience managing sales teams, expanding business, motivating, selling and training.

B.S.   Management, California State University.

ACCOMPLISHMENTS

—Motivated sales team to exceed quota by 24% when none of six other teams made quotas.

—Won Western Region Sales Award as director of district with highest volume (two years).

—Retrained four failing salesmen into efficient, organized producers who later earned promotions.

—Tripled base sales on part-time job as commission salesman while attending college. Won store sales award.

PREVIOUS EMPLOYMENT

District Sales Manager, Llago Wine Co., Los Angeles, 1975–1981. Managed 40-person sales team.

Manager, store operations, A&C Deli, Los Angeles, 1972–1975.

Salesman, AAA Stores, Los Angeles, 1969–1972. Sold women's shoes while attending college.

PERSONAL

Age 32 Married Two children Excellent health

Adapted from resume made available to author.

Tom Kandowski
497 Christy St.
Carteret, N.J. 07008
(201) 546-3876

WORK EXPERIENCE

ADMINISTRATIVE Coordinated plant service activities, including installation, maintenance and repair of equipment for data-processing center.

MECHANICAL Responsible for repairing and maintaining all mechanical aspects of railroad coal-dumper.

PIPEFITTING	Made extensive steam line alterations following conversion from coal to #6 oil firing of three boilers totaling 1250 h.p.
ELECTRICAL	Assisted electrical contractor in installing residential and industrial services.
STATIONARY ENGINEERING	Operated and maintained piston valve steam engines; maintained slide valve steam engines.

WORK HISTORY

1976–Present	Technicians, Inc., Maintenance Technician.
1973–1976	Northern Railroad. Oiler, Maintenance Mechanic.
1971–1973	Lewis Electric Co. Electrician's Assistant.

EDUCATION

B.S., Trenton State College. With honors.

Stationary Engineering, Middlesex County Vocational School. Blue-seal license.

Tom Jackson, "Resume Format," *National Business Employment Weekly,* August 23, 1981. [Resume reproduced in slightly abridged form.]

Rosemary Smith
536 Brompton Ave., Apt. 3-S
Chicago, Illinois 60657
Telephone (Residence) 312/472-3882
(Office) 312/267-6868, Ext. 570

OBJECTIVES

I have been an editor in textbook publishing for over ten years. Currently, I am project editor at Randolph College Publishing Co., where I am in charge of coordinating three college-level French projects and am responsible for supervising the personnel involved. In addition, I am involved in editing, production, and product development. Prior to being a project editor, I was a manuscript editor at Jackson Publishing for college-level French, education, and psychology texts. I entered publishing as an editor in the elementary/high school department of Elementary School Plus Publishing Co. I have two years of teaching experience at the eighth- and ninth-grade levels. I have a Magistere degree in French from the Sorbonne, an M.A.T. degree in French/Education from Brown University and a B.A. degree in French and Music from Randolph-Macon Woman's College.

EMPLOYMENT HISTORY

Present–3/76	Project Editor (college)	Randolph College Publishing Co.
2/76–4/73	Manuscript Editor (college)	Jackson Publishing Co.
3/73–6/69	Editor (el/hi)	Elementary School Plus Publishing Co.
6/69–9/67	French Teacher	Easton Junior High, Watertown, Mass.

Marian Faux, *The Complete Resume Guide* (New York: Monarch Press, 1980). [Resume reproduced in abridged form, slightly edited.]

THE COVER LETTER

The cover letter is the resume's traveling companion. Unless a resume only is requested, it should be accompanied by a letter. The latter may be just as important as the former. If skillfully drafted, the cover letter will make the reader want to give careful study to the resume.

The experts introduced earlier in this chapter offer these suggestions about cover letters:

Keep them short. Four paragraphs will often do. In the first paragraph say that you want to work for the company in question and mention the company *by name*. In the second, say what about the company appeals to you. (You may mention that you admire its marketing strategies, growth record, reputation for integrity, leadership position or some other positive characteristic. This is a time for flattery, but don't lay it on in gobs. Flattery is most transparent when applied in multiple coats.)

In paragraph three, say why you are qualified for the job you want. Give two or three reasons—if you have two or three really good ones. Don't contrive. Rely on demonstrated qualifications. And don't say you think you could help the company "turn things around." Telling a prospective boss you can teach him his business may be the surest way of guaranteeing you will never have him for a pupil.

In paragraph four, ask for an interview. Unless the company is in another city and your schedule is such that you can get there only on a certain date, don't say when you would like the interview. That is the prerogative of the prospective employer; you're only the prospective employee. But, if you haven't heard anything a week or two after mailing your resume and cover letter, make a phone call and ask politely if any consideration has been given to your request for an interview. It would not be inappropriate to mention in your cover letter that you will be making such a call.

Following is a cover letter of conventional format. It is from Marian Faux's *The Complete Resume Guide.*

Jeanette Beane
[Home address]
[Date]

Ms. Evelun Beckmann
Director of Cosmetics Development
Rosemont Cosmetics, Inc.
[Address]

Dear Ms. Beckmann:

This letter is to inquire about the possibility of obtaining work in cosmetics development at Rosemont Cosmetics.

I presently work for a competitive firm, where I am involved in the development of skin-care creams. I am aware of Rosemont's reputation for quality in the skin-care line, and because I am most interested in pursuing this line, I am especially eager to discuss the possibility of a senior research position at Rosemont.

I have ten years of experience in cosmetology and a doctorate from the Institute of Cosmetology in biochemistry. I was largely responsible for the development of my present employer's line of skin-care products, and I have some interesting ideas for new products.

Would it be possible for us to meet to discuss this further? I shall call your office early next week to inquire about an appointment.

Sincerely,

Jeanette Beane

You'll notice that Jeanette addressed Evelun Beckmann as Ms. Beckmann. This raises a problem of recent origin. Many women today prefer to be addressed as Ms. But some do not. The trick is to figure out which are which. And performing the trick successfully could be important if you want the woman in question to give you a job. If she is associated with feminist causes, you may offend her by calling her Miss or Mrs. If she is a more traditional woman, you may offend her by calling her Ms. It would be most helpful if women would indicate in their correspondence which form of address they prefer, for example by using a title parenthetically when signing off: "Sincerely, (Ms.) Evelun Beckmann." But that would cure the problem only when you already had correspondence from the woman. What to do when you haven't? I think it's important enough to warrant an inquiry before you write. I'd phone her company and ask the switchboard operator or a secretary how Evelun Beckmann prefers to be addressed. Even if you had to call long-distance, it could be worth it.

Before mailing a cover letter, make a copy of it. You may send many such letters before you're through. If you don't have copies, you may forget where many of them went, and when. You'll want to know how long it has been since you wrote Company X, so you'll know when it's time to make a follow-up call for an interview appointment.

If you've made such a call, and your request for an interview has been turned down, consider writing a thank-you note. At this point, I suspect, you have a question, and a good one: Thanks for what? The answer is thanks for whatever attention you've been given, even if it was only a minute on the telephone. ("I appreciated your taking time to talk with me today, and hope you'll have me in mind if any openings occur.") One of your objects is to develop a network of contacts, and the reader of that thank-you note could be one of them. If an opening should occur, your name might come to mind just because you took the trouble of saying thanks. I'll admit it's a long shot, but your only investment is the time it takes to write a one-paragraph note and the price of a postage stamp, a piece of stationery and an envelope.

YOUR CONTACT NETWORK

For the job hunter, communicating with people in writing is not as important as communicating with them in person. That doesn't mean the resumes and cover letters we've been talking about are unimportant. They can help set up in-person meetings with prospective employers. My point here is that you can't just mail out a hundred copies of your resume and then sit back expecting a hundred job offers. You've got to make personal contacts.

One way of doing this is by responding to employment advertisements in newspapers and other publications. You probably have sent your resume to some companies without even knowing if they have any openings. So you certainly shouldn't overlook openings announced in ads. Some of these will be blind ads, meaning that the employer is identified only by a box number. (Anonymity may be used because the employer has no intention of responding to most inquiries and would just as soon that a thousand applicants didn't know which company it was that wouldn't even give them the courtesy of a response.)

If the ad offers an attractive position, you'll have a lot of formidable competition. But follow the no-stone-unturned theory and apply anyway. Just keep in mind that you're in long-shot country when you go after a good job offered in a blind ad—or even in an open ad (in which the employer is identified). For job hunters, ads often don't add up to much.

The president of the personnel consulting firm of Camden and Associates in Hinsdale, Illinois, puts it this way: "People get employment offers by succeeding in the interview. Interviews are generated by personal contact ten times more often than by sending paper."[3]

Haldane Associates reported similar findings in charts based on two studies.[4] One study, published in 1974 by Harvard University sociologist Mark S. Granovetter, covered professional, technical and managerial workers who had recently found jobs.

A chart showed that 74.5 percent of them got their jobs by "informal" methods. Fewer than 10 percent got work by responding to ads and fewer than 9 percent got jobs through agencies. Haldane defined "informal" methods as "those whereby the job seekers exercise their own initiative in building personal contacts and making themselves known to potential employers."

The conclusion was that personal contacts "are of paramount importance in connecting people with jobs." Not only that, but "the best jobs, the ones with the highest pay and prestige and affording the greatest satisfaction to those in them, are most apt to be filled in this way."

A second study, published by the U.S. Department of Labor in 1975, covered 10.4 million persons who had found jobs, and showed that 63.4 percent of them had done so using informal methods. The study included not just executives and other white-collar employees, but all categories of wage and salary employees except farm workers. Fewer than 14 percent had found work through ads and only 12.2 percent through agencies. While the two studies are some years old, there is little reason to suppose the patterns have shifted appreciably.

This does not mean you should avoid employment agencies. If agencies find positions for 12.2 percent of 10.4 million applicants, they are finding more than a million jobs. One may be the job you're looking for.

Agencies (they like to be called personnel consulting services) typically charge their clients no fees. They are paid by employers who hire their clients. Employers are the agencies' customers.

One executive in the personnel consulting field has written: "Your best opportunity [of finding work] is through a personnel consulting service. Let them manage your job-hunting campaign for you. They are the experts. They have to be. They don't get paid unless they succeed."[5]

Signing up with an agency won't take much time, so you might wish to make it part of your reemployment strategy. But you would be ignoring the advice of many authorities if you did not make extensive use of informal job-hunting methods.

One of the most effective of the informal methods is to line up referral interviews. Haldane Associates defines the term:

"In the job-seeking process, there are two kinds of interviews: Referral Interviews and Job Interviews. When you are clearly being interviewed for a specific job, you are on a Job Interview. When you are building your contact network and are seeking advice and information about approaches to the right market for your capabilities, you are on a Referral Interview."

The idea is to talk to people not with the expectation that they will hire you but that they may be able to refer you to someone who will. Thomas M. Camden, the personnel consultant quoted earlier, calls this *networking* and describes it as "a highly effective way of generating interviews."

Networking takes time but is not difficult. It takes time because you want an elaborate network of contacts. You may find them through former employers, former business associates, friends, neighbors—anyone who knows people who may be able to put you in touch with employers in your field. Your insurance agent, for example, may have a policyholder who is an executive in your field. Your dentist may have patients who would be useful contacts. You may pick up leads at service club meetings or chamber of commerce functions.

Assuming you don't intrude excessively on their work schedules, most people will be quite willing to give you referral interviews. For one thing, you're not putting them under any pressure because you're not asking them to hire you. For another, they'll probably be flattered that you thought to come to them for counsel.

Some of them you will meet for the first time in your interviews. You will have been referred to them by friends or associates and will have written or phoned to set up interviews (enclosing your resume). Referral contacts may be useful even if they do not work in your field of interest. They may know someone in the field, or may be able to refer you to others with direct contacts.

A letter requesting a referral interview might begin:

Dear Ms. Llewellyn:

Our mutual friend, Sylvester Armbruster, suggested I contact you about the possibility of arranging a brief meeting to discuss my interest in a sales management position. Mr. Armbruster said you had mentioned recently that there were no openings in your company. But he thought you would be an excellent source of guidance. . . .

Suppose you get the interview with Llewellyn. Learn as much as you can about him and his company before you talk to him. That will indicate that you have an interest in him, and will encourage him to reciprocate.

When the conversation turns to your job-hunting campaign, be ready to give him a clear idea of what you want to do. Ask what his strategy would be if he were in your position. If he is familiar with your particular field of interest, ask about recent developments you may have missed. Inquire about job availability in different geographic areas. Be an informational vacuum cleaner, picking up every speck of intelligence that could be of any conceivable use to you.

At the end of the interview, ask Llewellyn if you can contact him again, to report any progress you've made and to inquire if anything further has occurred to him since you talked. Important: Ask if he can think of anyone else you should talk to. This is a proven method of expanding your contact network.

Finally, write a thank-you note after every referral interview.

"When you have had some practice," Haldane says, "you will discover that the referral approach will put you far ahead of most other job seekers. You will have interviews with people you never expected to contact."

Contact networks are useful not only to people who are out of work but to those who want to change jobs. For the unemployed, the bigger the network the better. The same rule may not apply, however, to those looking for a change of employment. The magazine *Industry Week* offered these words of caution:

"Seeking a change while still employed requires prudence. While the odds of landing an offer may increase in proportion to the number of people who know your intent, so does the danger that the news will get back to your boss.

"Experts recommend keeping the scale of clandestine job searches small, but intensive. The best way to do this, they advise, is to develop and use personal contacts: quietly leak word to a few friends on boards of directors; mention it to the president of your trade organization; ask a friend to call key people.

" 'But you've got to be careful,' warns Robert Lamalie, president of Lamalie Associates, Inc., a New York–based executive search firm. 'Pick only those people you trust absolutely.' "[6]

For a person who really wants to switch jobs, using the contact method may be worth the risks involved. Lamalie recognizes the value of such contacts for the same reason cited by others quoted in this chapter: because they account for the highest number of placements.

Nor are the advantages of networking available only to business executives and professionals. While the unemployed auto mechanic or gardener may not find it useful to send out resumes with cover letters asking for referral interviews, he can still use the techniques underlying the referral method. He can pass the word in much the same way, looking for contacts through friends, relatives, former employers, fellow lodge members—anybody who knows anybody.

Networking knows no age boundaries. It can be used by job hunters over fifty as easily as by people half their age—and perhaps even more easily because of the many years older workers have been accumulating contacts. Using such contacts was first on a list of techniques recommended by an over-fifty job seeker in a letter to the editor of a national employment publication. He said he still had not found a position after three months in the job market but had discovered that certain steps produced more promising responses than others and seemed sure to land him a job soon. His list of don'ts and do's:

"*I do not:*

"Apply to large, well-established companies. The slots they want to fill are filled by promotion from within and they rarely look at anyone our age.

"Register with agencies. They have too many younger people to offer to clients.

"Contact recruiting firms, for the same reason. . . .

"Send out unsolicited letters to lists of firms.

"*I do:*

"Contact friends and acquaintances to tell them of my availability.

"Answer selected ads that are particularly suited to my skills. This is not overly productive. I . . . get very few replies, but I get enough interviews to well justify the effort.

"Concentrate my efforts on smaller, growing companies who have to seek talent from the outside to fill growing needs or who do not have internal talent to fill needs.

"Contact service organizations, i.e., consulting firms, who actively seek mature, experienced individuals to provide expertise developed over the years. This has been a fruitful area for me, and age seems to be an asset rather than a liability. . . .

"Focus in specifically on positions and functions that I think my background well qualifies me for."[7]

THE JOB INTERVIEW

Sooner or later, your industry will pay off. You'll get a job interview. That does not mean, of course, that you've got a job. But it means you've got a job to do, to get ready for the interview.

Before each of your referral interviews, you'll recall, you made a point of learning something about the interviewer's company. You should do the same before a job interview, only your research should be more elaborate. If you've got a job interview set up with Company A, see if you can find the company's most recent annual report. Ask people with whom you've had referral interviews if they can give you any information about the company. Some firms print brochures or pamphlets about their operations; see if Company A does. Call the number listed for the company's administrative offices and ask the person on the switchboard whether such publications are available, and, if so, whether you could drop by and pick up copies.

With a little knowledge of the company, you may be able to answer questions more intelligently during your interview. And you may get ideas for a few questions of your own.

I remember the first interview I did for a head-coaching job. It was with President Earl Roadman and his board of directors at Morningside College in Iowa. When it appeared they had run out of questions, I pulled a piece of paper out of my pocket and inquired whether I could ask a few. I'd done my preinterview homework about the job and the school, but there were still a few things I wanted to know. I later got the job and Roadman told me they liked my approach in the interview. I was ready with some good questions. That was many years ago—in 1948– and I'm surprised I had enough insight that early in my career to recognize that a job interview should be a two-way reconnaissance. I'm also surprised I had enough guts. I had no job at the time, and none in sight.

Whatever you do, arrive for the interview on time. While you may want to be at Company A's offices fifteen minutes ahead of time, it's probably a good idea to make sure you're in the neighborhood even earlier. Give yourself an extra half hour to allow for the possibility of blowing a tire en route or getting cut off at a rail crossing by a mile-long freight train. If worse comes to worse yet, and you know you're going to be delayed despite your best efforts, get to a phone and call ahead, explaining your predicament and saying you'll be along at the earliest possible moment. Don't leave your interviewer waiting and wondering what happened to you.

If you want to make sure that nothing short of getting flattened by a falling meteor or stepping into an open manhole will make you late, you might consider a failsafe plan followed by some hypercautious law students at bar-examination time. They know that no excuse for being late is acceptable. The examination starts at the appointed hour come revolution in the streets or invasion from outer space. So they reserve rooms at a hotel in the vicinity of the exam site and check in at the hotel on the eve of the exam. If you're similarly anxiety-prone, you might see if there's a hotel or motel in Company A's neighborhood.

Let's assume that no calamities have befallen you, that you have arrived in plenty of time and are now entering the interviewer's office. What next?

George F. Stocks, our old friend from Chapter Four, passes on a couple of tips he picked up during his job-hunting campaign:

"When you go into an office and the interviewer asks you to sit down, don't immediately jump into a chair. Just stand where you are a moment and look around to see if you can find something attractive about the office. If you do, offer a compliment. But it should be sincere. If you don't see anything you think is particularly attractive, don't say anything.

"Another thing: Don't cross your arms in front of you. The interviewer may think you're a little bored with what he's saying. And don't clasp your fingers together, or your hands. Sit with your hands out in front of you, fingertips touching."

Unless your prospective employer operates a circus or a discotheque, forget about turning up for the interview in your fluorescent orange suit. Dress well but with restraint. You want to stand out from the crowd, but not as an eccentric. A brief story will illustrate the point:

"He seemed to have everything that a job hunter could want: intelligence, charm and one of corporate America's most prized credentials—a Harvard M.B.A. To distinguish himself from other applicants, however, he wore a baseball cap as well as a three-piece suit to his job interviews. He did indeed stick out— but he also struck out. Despite dozens of interviews, he got no offers.

"The problem, of course, was the cap, which sent recruiters the wrong message. Rather than marking him as a go-getting individualist, the hat told them that he lacked self-confidence and was overly concerned with image. Observes Harvard placement official Winn Price: 'Interviewers look for intellect, enthusiasm and a personality compatible with theirs.' "[8]

If you're like many people, you've got at least one nervous habit that gives away your discomfort in stressful situations. You may clear your throat unconsciously every eleven syllables or crack your knuckles or shift uneasily in your seat when asked a question. Your friends can probably help you identify such habits. Work at avoiding them. You might even sit in front of a mirror and do a practice interview, firing a tough question at yourself and making sure you give a twitchless response.

You've also got to work on the content of your responses. There is of course no way of anticipating every question an interviewer will ask you, but some questions are quite common, and can be quite difficult if tackled without preparation. You should get ready for them—not by trying to memorize answers word for word, but by getting the framework of your responses in mind.

Dave Lambert, a consultant with Haldane Associates, offers these examples of questions an interviewer might ask:

—Why do you want to work here?

—Why did you leave your last job?

—How long have you been out of work? What have you been doing all this time?

—What did you least like in your last job?

—If you could relive your last fifteen years, what changes would you wish to make?

—Tell me about your greatest disappointment in life.

—Have you done anything to improve yourself in the last year?

—Assuming we hire you, what do you see as your future?

—Everybody has pet peeves. What is yours?

—Are you considering other positions at this time? How does this one compare with them?

—Just what does success mean to you? How do you judge it?

—Everybody likes to criticize. What do people criticize about you?

—What do you generally find to criticize in most people?

—Tell me about yourself.

—What are some of your weaknesses or failures?

You could be asked many of these questions or only a few. You could be asked many others. The list is not intended to be exhaustive. And there are no pat answers. But Haldane Associates furnishes these tips:

"Your answers must be worked out carefully and intelligently. To help create the best impression and minimize the difficulties resulting from careless answers, remember these general principles: Listen to the question. Understand exactly what is asked. If you are unsure, ask for clarification. Take time to think through all the facts which should be used to answer the question. Then use *positive information* to answer the question directly and to the point. . . . Be truthful. But it is not necessary to offer unsolicited information which could detract from the image you are creating."

Before you go to an interview, put yourself in the interviewer's chair and make up a list of questions he or she might ask a person like you. Then answer them and store the gist of the answers in your memory bank.

Let's take one of the broadest "questions" on Lambert's sample list: "Tell me about yourself." It's so open-ended that it almost invites a recitation of your life history. Decline the invitation.

If unprepared for such a question, you may find yourself embarked on an aimless and seemingly endless response. "Well," you might begin, "I was born in Tillamook, Oregon, and my first ambition was to be a steeplejack because I had an uncle who installed tile on church steeples—until he stepped back one day to admire his work—but then I got a lead part in our senior play in high school and decided to go on Broadway but my first job was actually repairing tires at a truck stop and then I met a tree surgeon who got me interested in eucalyptus diseases and . . ."

One of many ways to improve on that answer would be to tell the interviewer things about yourself that relate to the job you want. You might say, "Well, one of the most pertinent things I could tell you about myself is that I have been thinking for some time of obtaining a sales position with your company because it is one of the leaders in the field. And I think my resume shows that I have had both the experience and success needed to qualify for such a job. I've always liked selling. I guess it's because I tend to get along with most people and like taking on challenges. . . ."

In addition to personal inquiries, you may be asked questions designed to test your problem-solving ability. An interviewer may mention an actual problem facing his company and ask how you would go about solving it. The best approach is not to try to come up with a solution on the spot. First, the answer may be worth no more than the amount of thought you gave it. Second, offering an instant solution may leave the impression that you're given to impulsive responses. An alternative is to say your experience has been that problems require individual attention and often a good deal of thought. Then, to illustrate your experience, mention one or two problems you encountered on a previous job and explain how you overcame them.

For reasons I will leave to others to try to justify, women job applicants have to be ready for some questions men needn't worry about. For example:

—What child-care arrangements have you made?
—How does your husband feel about your working?
—How do you feel about attending conferences with men?
—Do you think you can supervise men?
—This job has always been handled by a man. Do you think you can handle it?
—Why do you want to work?
—How do you feel about "women's liberation"?
—Would your strength or independence scare men?

Whatever the woman applicant may think of sex-related questions, she must realistically be ready to answer them, within limits. Some such questions are unnecessary, even insulting. If a woman thinks she is being denied a job solely because of her sex, she may have good reason not only to be offended but to lodge a complaint with the Equal Employment Opportunity Commission. She is not entitled to a job just because she is a woman. But she is entitled to fair consideration.

What if you were fired from your last job and are asked why you left? Disemployees of both sexes should handle this the same way: Tell the truth.

Having been fired certainly doesn't make you a more desirable job candidate. But it doesn't make you unemployable, either. I have furnished living proof of that.

One thing that will definitely make you a more desirable candidate is an appreciation of your interviewer's interests. Many interviewees fail in this area. Haldane Associates explains:

"In the traditional job interview, the applicant's purpose usually is to get the job, while the potential employer's purpose is to find a solution to his or her own problem. Sometimes these two purposes are on a collision course and block communication. Often applicants are so focused on their own needs that they fail to perceive the interviewer's. In other cases job seekers sit back and let the interviewer control the interview. The result is an unproductive interview. You cannot make a strong and useful presentation of your capabilities if you ignore the needs of the interviewer. . . . If you are focused solely on your own problem, such as the need to become employed and to produce an income, you can never feel or show a real interest in your interviewer."

One way of avoiding such focus is to go into the interview, not with the idea of coming away with a job offer that day, but of establishing good rapport with the interviewer.

"If you free yourself from the pressure of having to 'make the sale' on this first interview," Haldane says, "you will find it much easier to concentrate on making an impression that will assure a second interview. More than one interview is [usually] needed to get a good job offer, so it is unrealistic to expect one on the first interview. Instead, the goal of the initial job interview is to get a second interview."

Important: Write a thank-you note after the first one and tell the interviewer you are looking forward to a second meeting. Also make a point of being courteous to the interviewer's secretary and learning her name. My secretary would sometimes drop casual, complimentary remarks about people who had been particularly polite to her. That made a positive impression on me, and I've tried to put the idea into practice. It can make it easier for you to get to see the boss the next time. Even if it doesn't, it's a nice courtesy to cultivate.

I was invited to the White House once for a brief visit with President Reagan. I did not get to meet his secretary, Helene von Damme, before the visit, but I arranged to spend a couple of minutes with her before leaving. As chairman of the President's Council on Physical Fitness and Sports, I could have occasion to call the White House. And the president's secretary might at least remember I made a point of meeting her. I think it's a good idea to go out of your way to thank a secretary when leaving an office. It can't hurt you, and it could help. At worst, you will have the satisfaction of having made a nice gesture.

In any interview, bear in mind that the interviewer is not only forming opinions about your qualifications but also sizing you up as a person. Do you seem to be a person who could work well with others, who would "fit in"? The interviewer is probably looking for a team player—not a robot who will perform any function without question, but a person willing to sacrifice some personal interests for the good of the overall enterprise.

A sound approach is to borrow a thought from the late John F. Kennedy. Rather than asking what the company can do for you, talk about what you can do for the company. Haldane Associates says it has learned from thirty years in career counseling "that it is not necessarily the most qualified candidate who gets the job but [may instead be] the most *constructive,* the most enthusiastic and the most cooperative."

Much the same point has been made by other experts. For example:

John Artise, placement director at Adelphi University on Long Island, believes that personality counts more than anything else in the job hunt. The forceful and personable Artise, 32, reached this conclusion after seven years of first-hand research masquerading as an applicant for some three hundred jobs. Once, when he mentioned to a potential employer that he played chess, the man pulled out a board and challenged him to a game. (Artise declined the match.) In all, Artise got offers from roughly two-thirds of the companies for positions as disparate as copy editor and biochemist. A manufacturer of office machines was willing to pay him $33,000 a year to be the firm's marketing manager for Spain. "They're not buying your credentials," Artise says. "They're buying you."[9]

From personal experience, I know how a job interviewer tries to size up an applicant's personality, looking for signs of a constructive attitude. In Washington, I was general manager as well as head coach of the Redskins and interviewed everyone hired by the club. In 1973, I was looking for an assistant coach to handle our special teams and interviewed Paul Lanham, who had been an assistant with the St. Louis Cardinals. He came to my home in McLean, Virginia, and did an exceptional job of selling himself.

I always looked for people who were hard workers and displayed innovation, who wanted to do something more than was being done by everybody else in the National Football League. At the end of the interview I would ask the person interviewed to send me a letter, explaining how he could improve our special teams or public relations or whatever part of the organization he would be working with.

Lanham went from my house to catch a plane at Dulles Airport. He was delayed for some reason. Instead of just sitting around the airport, he went back to the hotel where he had been staying and wrote his letter there. Then he called and told me he was having the letter delivered to my home.

I like self-starters and that really impressed me. What the letter would say was less important to me than the ingenuity he showed by taking advantage of his delay at the airport. As it turned out, the letter had some good ideas in it. And Lanham had a job.

I had hired another special-teams coach in 1968, while still in Los Angeles. We had just lost a game to the Chicago Bears by one point, and our special teams were partly to blame. Up to then I had assigned various coaches to work with the special teams in addition to handling their regular jobs. I decided we needed one man to devote himself to the special teams full-time.

What I wanted was a highly organized person who could motivate. The special teams would be practicing longer, and we needed someone who could sell them on the importance of their function and get them to put in that extra time productively.

A young coach then with Stanford came in for an interview. I knew after five minutes that he could handle the job, but I didn't offer it to him right away. I needed assurance that he really wanted it. He would be the last man on the staff and would not be making as much as the other assistants. So I told him to think about it and give me a call.

He did, and I could tell that he had what I was looking for: enthusiasm. He wasn't just willing to take the job; he was raring to take it. I could tell he would hit the ground with his legs pumping.

Someone capable of performing a job but not excited about it is a good bet to get bored before long. That didn't happen to this coach. He did an outstanding job. He would later become a head coach and take the Philadelphia Eagles to the Super Bowl. Dick Vermeil was his name.

Don't get the idea that you should never do an interview if you're not excited about a job opening. I've interviewed for many jobs that didn't look very exciting. I do it for two reasons. First, the more you interview, the more you learn about the process. Second, you never know when a job that appears uninteresting at first glance may become more appealing on further inspection. If it does, you can then make your enthusiasm apparent.

Up to now, you may have noticed, nothing has been said about the point at which salary should be discussed in a job interview. Nothing was said earlier because it's not a subject that should be brought up early, at least not by the applicant.

Rule: Never talk money until the interviewer has made it clear you're wanted for the job. Some interviewers may not mind. But the one you're talking to may.

In 1971, my first year with the Redskins, I was looking for a conditioning coach. I didn't know of any club that had such a coach working full-time, but that's what I wanted. I thought it might give us an edge.

I interviewed one person who came highly recommended and seemed to be just the man I was looking for—until the interview. He made the mistake of bringing up salary very early in our conversation. It cost him the job. I guess it was because I had made a point of never taking a job just for the money involved. In fact, I've accepted some jobs when it meant taking a cut in pay.

I'm not suggesting that money is irrelevant, or that a person should never ask for more than is offered. I left the Redskins partly because of a disagreement over money. But money is one of two things I think a job applicant should avoid bringing up early in an interview. (The other is that feeble conversational crutch, the weather, a topic most unlikely to excite the prospective employer unless he or she is looking for a meteorologist.) I like a person whose first interest in joining an organization is in wanting to share in its achievements, not in knowing where to find the pay window.

Even when it's clear the interviewer wants you for the job, let him be the first to mention a salary figure. He probably has a figure in mind, or a range of figures within which he can negotiate. If you name a figure first, you expose yourself to at least two risks. You may ask for less than the interviewer is prepared to offer. (A revolting thought, you'll agree.) Or you may ask for more than the maximum he can offer. This will put you in the awkward position of having to back down or decline the job. And, in the interviewer's eyes, you may have become at least a somewhat troublesome person.

If the interviewer asks you to name a figure first, put the ball right back in his court by saying, "I'd rather defer to the company and have you tell me what you have in mind." He may return the ball to your side by asking, "Well, how much would you need to live on?" Tell him you want to be paid what you're worth, not what you need.

This doesn't necessarily mean you're going to accept anything he offers. If he mentions a figure substantially less than you think the job should pay, don't say anything. Look thoughtful. This is a diplomatic way of informing him (a) that you're thinking it over and (b) that you're not thrilled by the amount offered.

"Remember," Haldane says, "that the interviewer has already made a commitment to you and is now in a 'buying' position. In better than 50 percent of all negotiating situations where silence has been used, the interviewer will mention a higher figure without further discussion."

But suppose he doesn't. If you want the job badly, you might accept the first offer with the understanding that your salary will be reviewed in six months or so.

In any event, never accept an offer on the spot. Give yourself a day to consider it. You may think of some questions you need answered before taking the job. The interviewer won't mind waiting twenty-four hours for an answer. He knows you're making an important decision and understands the professional way to make it is with deliberation. Being professional might even help you later. Haldane says many job applicants who "handled themselves well during their salary negotiations were treated with greater respect and were given more opportunities to advance."

As if getting a job wasn't already enough of an ordeal, some companies have made it even more agonizing by asking applicants to take lie-detector tests. *Business Week* magazine said a 1978 survey showed that 20 percent of the nation's largest companies used polygraph tests to check out background information and otherwise test the honesty of job applicants.[10]

Such tests are forbidden by law in several states. Even where permitted, they must be voluntary. Employers cannot force you to take a polygraph exam as a condition of employment; but they can ask.

If you say yes, be prepared to answer whether you have ever used drugs, ever committed a serious undetected offense, ever stolen from an employer. Answer the last question yes even if you never took anything more valuable than pencils or notepads. Otherwise, you may get a "tendency toward deception" reading on the polygraph machine.

One executive who submitted to a lie-detector test called it "the most humiliating thing I've ever gone through." Others dismissed the experience as just another of the hoops a person must jump through in the interest of career advancement.

An exam takes about forty-five minutes. It is usually given at a polygraph examiner's office.

One examiner says it does no good to try to finesse the exam by taking a tranquilizer beforehand. "Your nervous system will override its effect," he says, "and everyone is [expected to be] nervous except hardened criminals or psychotics."

Some employers also inflict a form of torture known as the "stress interview." It's a "tough-question" session. Thomas M. Camden, one of the authors quoted earlier, describes this interview as "a technique used by uninformed interviewers to ascertain an applicant's ability to cope with pressure situations."

"Stress interviews seldom work," Camden says. "The only value they have is to convince the applicant not to work for a company that permits such stupid practices."

But job applicants also are guilty of occasional excesses. A *New York Post* column for job hunters told the story of a woman who went to an employment agency with the right credentials but the wrong attitude:

"The applicant (we'll call her Anna) . . . was highly belligerent to the receptionist. 'Why do I have to fill out another one of these things?' Anna was referring to the application. 'All they do is keep you waiting and waiting,' she said to another job candidate. She generated negative intensity in the interviewing room.

"Anna is a secretary in mid-life, has excellent skills and is self-supporting. She is angry. After five months, all she is getting is 'small talk' and advice to 'relax,' she says. 'It's a waste of time coming here because you can't place me. The companies don't want to pay my salary. They all want young, good-looking girls.' . . . Anna [was] employed for fifteen years by the same company, was highly comfortable in her position of authority. . . . She worked in an office where she ruled the roost and had become demanding and overbearing."[11]

Anna had no idea how to dress for an interview. She would turn up in designer jeans, a brilliantly colored tight blouse, open-back disco shoes and no stockings. Her hair and nails were not groomed.

Early in her interviews she would ask about fringe benefits, days off, raises and vacations. She didn't want interviewers wasting her time if they didn't have all the right goodies to offer.

"Anna might not be getting a position because of her own self-image," the column said. "She wonders, Who would want to hire me? She actually rejects the company before they have a chance to reject her. . . .

"With Anna's skills, we can place her in a good job. With Anna's attitude, no one can place her."

1. Marian Faux, *The Complete Resume Guide* (New York: Monarch Press, 1980).
2. Tom Jackson, "Resume Format," *National Business Employment Weekly,* August 23, 1981. Adapted from *The Perfect Resume* (New York: Anchor Books/Doubleday, 1981).
3. Thomas M. Camden, "Out of Work Terms," *National Business Employment Weekly,* August 23, 1981.
4. "How People Get Jobs," produced for Bernard Haldane Associates, Boston, 1977.
5. Jules Beitler, executive director, Association of Personnel Consultants of New York State, "On the Job Front," *New York Post,* July 14, 1980.
6. Bruce Jacobs, "Job-Hunting on the Sly," *Industry Week,* March 9, 1981.
7. John Wagner, Glen Rock, New Jersey; Letters to the Editor, *National Business Employment Weekly,* August 23, 1981.
8. Malcolm N. Carter, "A Sharpshooter's Guide to the Job Hunt," *Money,* June 1981.
9. Malcolm N. Carter, "A Sharpshooter's Guide to the Job Hunt."
10. Donald H. Dunn, "Personal Business," *Business Week,* July 27, 1981.
11. "On the Job Front," *New York Post,* September 15, 1980. [Information in column furnished by Association of Personnel Consultants of New York State.]

8 / *Where to Find a Job*

READING UP

You may really be looking at two kinds of "wheres" when you face the question of where to look for a job. George F. Stocks, the auto-parts man we met in Chapter Four, found the job opportunity he was looking for by reading books in a library. Others track down jobs by reading ads in newspapers and magazines. If we needed a fancy name for the process, we could call it the "bibliographical search."

But you may also find yourself engaged in a "geographical search." Let's say you've been reading and networking and sending out resumes, and your labor has paid off. You've landed three job offers. But all are from companies outside your immediate area. In fact, the nearest is three states away. You must now consider not only what you want to do but where you want to do it. The second consideration may be as important as the first. But before we discuss geography, let's return a moment to bibliography.

For supplement to this chapter, see Appendix.

The U.S. Government Printing Office in Washington publishes a useful directory called *The Dictionary of Occupational Titles* (commonly referred to as the D.O.T.). It's available in many libraries. Among other things, it lists thousands of job titles, briefly describes duties normally associated with each job and tells you which businesses and industries use which job titles.

The D.O.T. has a supplement called *Entry Occupational Classifications*. This is a good book to consult if you have little or no experience to sell an employer in your field of interest.

Industrial directories also may be found in many libraries. Among those you might want to check are Poor's *Register of Corporations,* Standard & Poor's *Industrial Index,* Dun & Bradstreet's *Million Dollar Directory* and *Middle Market Directory* and Thomas's *Register of American Manufacturers.* These books list thousands of companies, giving their locations, describing their products or services and identifying their officers.

While in the library, you might look for a couple of helpful nondirectory books: *How to Get the Job That's Right for You,* by Ben Greco, and *What Color Is Your Parachute?* by Richard Nelson Bolles.

Two magazines I've long enjoyed are *Forbes* and *Fortune.* I'm especially impressed by *Forbes,* both because of its overall content and the detail in its stories. A person looking for a job may also find valuable information in such magazines as *Business Week, Business World, Money, Barron's, Newsweek* and *Time.* Among newspapers, of course, the *Wall Street Journal* has no peer in the field of business news. But informative stories about jobs and business trends may also be found in the *New York Times, Washington Post, Los Angeles Times* and other major newspapers. In addition to stories, they often carry employment ads in their financial sections. And, of course, they carry many help-wanted ads in their classified sections. Read the classifieds, but don't count on them as your most likely source of deliverance.

Trade magazines and newspapers are another good source of information. Some offer in-depth coverage of particular fields and, if nothing else, will help you identify the leading companies in a given field and learn something about them.

If you neither subscribe to nor read any of the publications just mentioned, you probably still have one useful book at hand. Depending on the size of the town you live in, your Yellow Pages list from hundreds to tens of thousands of employers. And they're all classified by type of business. There's no better place to get a quick rundown on potential local employers in your field of interest.

If you need a little more information about a particular company, the chamber of commerce may be helpful. And it may be helpful in another way: Many chambers hold mixers—parties at which business people get together. If you can crash one, you may make some good contacts.

Better Business Bureaus are not good primary sources of employment information. But you might consider consulting them if you have an interest in—or an offer from—a company you don't know much about. If you've just lost one job, you don't want to risk another big setback by hiring on with a company that has a poor reputation and perhaps an equally poor life expectancy.

Many if not all states have manufacturers' associations that may be able to provide statewide listings of companies in different fields. They may also publish useful newsletters.

If you've voted in five or more presidential elections, you might consider joining a Forty-Plus Club. There's probably one in your area if you live in or near a fairly large city. Forty-Plus Clubs do a superior job of locating potential employers for forty-plus people.

Other clubs may help you even if finding jobs for people is not one of their intended functions. Let's say you've just lost a job on which you met a person who got you to join a service club. Your inclination, as I mentioned in an earlier chapter, is probably to avoid embarrassment by avoiding people. So you may have stopped attending the club's meetings. If so, you've probably made a mistake. Chances are many members of the club are business people—people you can use in your networking campaign. Turn up at the next meeting even if it means swallowing a little pride along with that rubber chicken they serve for lunch.

THE JOB OUTLOOK

"While unemployment lines lengthen . . . many well-paid jobs in America go unfilled for lack of qualified applicants."

I read that not long ago in *Nation's Business.*

"Many of these job openings are in fields that will provide the greatest employment opportunities for the next ten years," the story continued. "Employment in almost all occupations is expected to increase at a rate of about 21% in the next decade. Some occupations, however, are expected to grow at least 50%. They include bank clerks and officers, financial managers, business-machine repairers, computer service technicians, dental assistants and hygienists, flight attendants, guards, landscape architects, nurses, podiatrists, therapists and travel agents."[1]

The outlook is somewhat less promising for lawyers, biologists, oceanographers, key punch operators, research workers, teachers and bakers, the story said. But it offered this optimistic forecast by Harold P. Fowler, associate director of the University of Michigan career planning and placement office: "If you are willing to go where the jobs are, there is usually no trouble getting a job in your college major or a related field."

That may not sound very reassuring if you don't happen to have a college major. But a person who has acquired skills by on-the-job experience also may be in an advantageous position, if he is mobile.

The *Nation's Business* story drew predictions from *The Occupational Outlook Handbook,* published by the Department of Labor. Updated every two years, the handbook forecasts changes for the coming ten years in 250 occupations monitored by the department's Bureau of Labor Statistics.

The predictions are of course not guaranteed. *Nation's Busi-*

ness quoted one expert who says such forecasts cannot be made with great confidence. Still, the story said, "the handbook remains a good guide for career planning" and is used in many schools.

"The number of workers employed in any job depends on the demand for the goods and services provided by those workers," the magazine said. "However, changes in technology have brought about exceptions. While more books are being bound now than ever before, job opportunities in binderies are limited because mechanized bookbinding has reduced the need for workers. Employment also has been affected by changes in business practices. Despite heavy use of credit by consumers, employment of credit managers has declined because retailers have centralized credit operations."

Another engaging point: More jobs open up because of people leaving the work force than because of economic growth. This means fields that are growing only slowly but that employ large numbers of people will provide more new jobs than small, rapidly growing fields. Those in high-turnover positions include accountants, bookkeeping workers, cashiers, real estate brokers and retail salespersons.

The *Nation's Business* story offered ten-year projections for a number of fields:

High technology—"Computer science should remain one of the hottest job areas well into the future. . . . While increased application of high technology is expected to provide jobs throughout the country, there will continue to be heavy concentrations in some areas. [One source] says New England, California and Texas will continue as major centers."

Business management—"Arthur Letcher, director of graduate corporate placement for the Wharton School at the University of Pennsylvania, . . . sees the greatest opportunities occurring in expanding companies, especially those moving into international markets. At the same time, he says, California will continue rapid growth while growth will remain steady in such areas as Chicago, St. Louis and much of Texas. Consultants of all types, he predicts, will be in even greater demand than now. Also in increasing demand are executives with training in labor, industrial and government relations.''

Health care—''There are now more than 4.5 million workers in health-related fields, only 38 percent of whom are doctors and nurses. The remainder are in the growing classifications of allied health professionals, a broad category that includes respiratory therapy workers, electrocardiograph technicians, emergency medical technicians, laboratory, X-ray and operating room technicians, and practical nurses. . . . The outlook is also bright for dental assistants.''

Engineering—''The entire field . . . is expected to experience faster-than-average growth in the next decade, with 46,500 openings for new engineers each year. The Bureau of Labor Statistics says that the greatest number of job openings will be for electrical, industrial, civil, mechanical and aerospace engineers. . . . Growth is expected to be particularly strong in energy-related areas [and in] chemical and environmental engineering.''

Science—'' 'The job market will be good for geologists,' says Betty Vetter [executive director of the Scientific Manpower Commission], 'particularly those in petroleum geology.' Chemistry, she says, continues to be a good field, and since there is no longer the big oversupply of physicists that there was a few years ago, job prospects there have greatly improved. Astronomers, however, will find little chance for employment, and the biology field is overcrowded.''

Law—'' 'It's an expanding market,' says Richard S. Collins, a spokesman for the American Bar Association. 'Young lawyers are not causing the litigation explosion—they are responding to it.' . . . Nevertheless, he says, 'There is no question that there are a large number of students in the country's law schools, and more law schools are being accredited every day, so competition will be tight.' ''

Banking—''Job opportunities . . . are expected to grow more rapidly than usual because banks are expanding their services, and increased use of computers has added to the need for trained executives.''

Sales—"Sales occupations of all types are expected to provide an increasing number of jobs in the coming decade, including an annual need for 226,000 retail sales workers, 50,000 real estate agents and brokers, 40,000 wholesalers and 21,700 manufacturers' representatives."

Education—"Jobs for kindergarten and elementary school teachers are expected to grow at about the average rate. At the secondary school level, competition for jobs will be keen, but those qualified to teach special education, vocational subjects, mathematics and the natural and physical sciences will find more favorable job opportunities. The outlook is not bright for college and university faculty members . . . because of both decreasing enrollments and budgetary constraints."

Government—"Government, a major provider of jobs in the fields already mentioned and many others during the 1960s, seems to have leveled off during the 1970s and can no longer be considered a growth industry for the 1980s."

Some of the same ground was covered by an earlier article in *Money* magazine. The *Money* story offered some good detail in several areas, including:

Health care—"Improvements in diet and medical care have lengthened the average life span of Americans by ten years since 1940, rapidly altering the demographics of age. The sixty-five-and-over group is growing about twice as fast as the population as a whole. By 1990 there will be about three million more people at the high end of the age spectrum—seventy-five and older—than there are today.

"These 'old-olds,' more than the 'young-olds' (aged fifty-five to seventy-five), are prone to illness. . . . A study made for the Rand Corporation, a California think tank, indicates a need for eight thousand to nine thousand geriatric specialists by 1990 and twenty thousand by the turn of the century."

High technology—"To put almost any kind of talent to work in the eighties will require an understanding of computers and what they can do. 'People have to realize that they are going to be information workers,' says Paul Shay of SRI [a California research firm]. Young people have to abandon any fears they may have of the new technology and learn to use its tools. 'Information will be the new source of wealth,' says Shay. 'The distinction used to be between the haves and the have-nots. In the eighties, it will be between the knows and the know-nots.' "[2]

In an article on employment prospects for women, the magazine *Glamour* presented a list of "jobs with great growth potential, 1978–1990."[3] The projections were based on information from the U.S. Department of Labor. Here is the list (with expected percent of increase in parentheses):

Occupational therapists (100), computer service technicians (92.5), speech pathologists and audiologists (87.5), dental hygienists (85.7), homemaker-home health aides (70.0), industrial machine repairers (66.0), dining room attendants and dishwashers (62.8), licensed practical nurses (62.2), travel agents (62.2), lithographers (61.1), mining engineers (58.3), health service administrators (57.1), flight attendants (56.2), business machine repairers (56.0), respiratory therapists (55.0), bank officers and financial managers (54.5), podiatrists (53.7), city managers (52.0), nursing aides, orderlies and attendants (52.0), teacher aides (51.8), bank clerks (50.5), dental assistants (50.0), physical therapists (50.0), hotel housekeepers and assistants (49.9), cashiers (49.7), registered nurses (49.6), dental lab technicians (48.9), landscape architects (45.8), secretaries and stenographers (45.4).

(For a more comprehensive look at the Labor Department projections, see Appendix. It presents forecasts of future demand for workers in hundreds of fields.)

These demand estimates were made by experts. But, like long-range weather forecasts, they should be viewed with caution. Any such calculations can be thrown off by unforeseeable events.

"It might be argued," one writer has suggested, "that professional and technical careers involve a kind of inescapable dice roll. A young person contemplating any such career is, of course, looking at very long lead times: it can take four years or more between the time he makes the career decision and the time he's actually ready to go to work.

"But the forecasts about future demand for trained professionals have been notoriously wide of the mark. During the last year or so, it happens, engineering graduates have been in clover: the defense boom, the basically strong showing of technology-intensive industries in the U.S. and our failure to produce enough engineering graduates in the 1970s have combined to create an explosive demand for those who are now graduating.

"The supply-demand balance is extremely favorable to them because in the mid-1970s the job market for engineers was discouraging."[4]

Future demand for nonprofessionals may be no more predictable. But many of them have done comparatively well financially in recent years, as noted in a recent *Forbes* article:

"It was not so long ago that high school counselors routinely told every kid that he or she ought to go to college and become a professional, perhaps like the counselor. That was good advice until the counselor started noticing that the fellow tuning his car was making more than a teacher. Census data show that by 1978 starting salaries for vocational school grads were only 6 percent below those of college graduates. A decade earlier the difference was 24 percent."[5]

Another article reported similar findings:

"Many people think that they must go to college to find a good job. But, according to Dr. Daniel B. Dunham, HEW's deputy commissioner of occupational and adult education, '80 percent of the jobs in this country don't require a degree from a four-year college.'

"In fact, students with technical training from business, trade or other vocational schools often find better-paying jobs than do college graduates. . . . Twenty years ago, trade schools were geared primarily to men entering agricultural or industrial jobs. Now they prepare both sexes for jobs in many fields—from nursing and home economics to sales and computer science. Presently, over seventeen million men and women are enrolled in vocational programs throughout the country."[6]

JOBS AND GEOGRAPHY

Population trends are another key to where the action will be in the job market. Like demand for workers in a given field, these trends cannot be predicted with certainty. But the Bureau of the Census has prepared state-by-state population-change projections for 1980–1990.

The top ten probable leaders (with projected gains in parentheses): Florida (27.1%), Arizona (27.0), Colorado (20.8), Nevada (20.8), Alaska (19.2), Utah (18.9), Idaho (18.8), New Mexico (17.4), Texas (16.3), Wyoming (16.2).

The bottom ten: District of Columbia (−5.0), New York (0.5), Ohio (2.3), Pennsylvania (2.6), Illinois (3.6), Indiana (4.2), Connecticut (4.7), Iowa (4.8), South Dakota (4.9), Kansas (5.4).

The expected growth leaders, you'll notice, are mostly states with a lot of growing room. There has been a parallel development at the local level. Rural towns are attracting more people than big cities.

For nearly two centuries, the shift in U.S. population was from rural to urban areas. Then, in the 1970s, it turned around. While now moving from big towns to small, the population continues to shift from east to west. In 1790, the U.S. center of population was twenty-three miles east of Baltimore. By 1850 it was in West Virginia, about to move into Ohio. By 1900 it was well into a half-century-long crawl through Indiana, and by 1950 it was in Illinois. By 1980 it had moved on to Missouri and, for the first time, was west of the Mississippi. When last seen, it was still headed west.

Many of the westward bound were headed for small towns. As indicated by a *Money* magazine report I came across not long ago, Americans have begun to think small when it comes to deciding where to live.

"In the seventies," the report said, "about four million people migrated from the northeastern and north-central states to the southern and western states, regions that now account for more than half of the country's population—and most of its rapidly rising small cities. That movement is expected to continue into the eighties, though people will favor Rocky Mountain highs to Sunbelt tans. Energy-related industries in the mountain states will be a major source of new jobs. . . . Nine of the ten states expected to grow the fastest are involved to some extent in energy production: Arizona, Colorado, Alaska, Nevada, Utah, Idaho, New Mexico, Texas and Wyoming. . . .

"The job trends of the past decade are also predicted to continue into the 1980s. 'Seventy-five percent of all additional jobs will be created in the South and West, and the high point of concentration will be in the small cities,' says George Sternlieb, director of the Center for Urban Policy at Rutgers University. Many of these jobs will be the highly skilled, highly paid and highly portable ones associated with advanced-technology fields.'"[7]

Generally, today's ambitious smaller cities want to get bigger without getting a lot dirtier. They don't want to look like our older industrial cities. They want low-pollution industries.

The bigger they get, of course, the more big-city problems they'll have. More congestion, for example, and probably more crime. But they're not likely to see commuter traffic reduced to the state of paralysis in which it is customarily found in New York and Los Angeles.

"Although they may grow up to have some of the same difficulties of their larger cousins," the *Money* report said, "small cities face a generally rosy future. That's because they are likely to stay relatively small. There are lots of them to divide up the refugees from the big urban centers. In the next ten years many of those in the forefront of this demographic movement will reach their forties, a time when people are usually less inclined to push on. Even so, most members of the baby-boom generation are still in their twenties and haven't yet decided where they want to spend the rest of their working and playing life. The lure of the small cities is strong enough that the march should go on for some time to come."

The *Money* report included a story about ten cities rated among the best of the country's growing smaller urban centers. Factors considered included probable job-growth rate, quality of schools, accessibility to colleges or universities, state tax rates and scenic qualities.

"Many of these cities score high in all categories," the report said, "and none misses out in more than one. Most are regional hubs, with diversified opportunities in manufacturing, sales, health and communications. Professional and managerial jobs are plentiful, although women may have a harder time moving onto and up the executive ladder than they do in larger cities."[8]

The ten: Fort Collins, Colorado (whose larger neighbors include the Rockies and whose larger employers include Eastman-Kodak, Hewlett-Packard and Teledyne Water Pik); Sioux Falls, South Dakota (an agricultural and banking center in a state whose citizens have the longest average life span in the country); San Angelo, Texas (which counts the nation's largest wool market among the main elements in a diverse economy); Appleton, Wisconsin (home of Kleenex and about 60,000 people who still like to live by traditional values); Sarasota, Florida (which has a thriving tourist industry and claims to have more golf courses per capita than any other U.S. city); Nashua, New Hampshire (a fine old mill town with some big new employers, including Digital Equipment, Sanders Associates, Teledyne Electromechanisms and Nashua Corporation); Billings, Montana (once the home of Calamity Jane, now a growing energy center); Lafayette, Louisiana (a good restaurant town in which more than 750 petroleum-connected companies have established offices); Knoxville, Tennessee (a big small city with excellent schools, a varied economy and an enduring love for University of Tennessee football); Olympia, Washington (center of a fast-growing metropolitan area surrounded by marvelous scenery).

I thought the list might be useful if you happen to be shopping around. I understand, of course, that these cities may not be for you. I'm not suggesting that everybody pack up by next Thursday and head for a small city because that's where the action seems to be going. The entire population of New York State need not be evacuated to Wyoming because the growth rate is higher out there.

In the 1980–1990 population projections I cited a little earlier, you may remember, Wyoming was among the leaders (with an expected increase of 16.2 percent) and New York was the state expected to gain the least (0.5 percent). I'm sure I won't be the first to tell you numbers can be hazardous if not handled carefully. For example, if New York State should gain only 0.5 percent in population, it would acquire more new residents than Wyoming would by gaining 16.2 percent. Just because a state is not among the projected leaders in population growth does not mean you can't find the job you want there. There may be more jobs of the particular type you want in New York than in the fastest-growing state in the country.

Another point before leaving the numbers: You may recall the Census Bureau projections indicated the population of the District of Columbia would decline by 5 percent in the 1980s. Maybe so, but watch out for a number like that. It tells you only what population change is expected within the district proper, and not within the greater Washington area. Central-city population figures may be misleading. The last time I looked, for example, Columbus, Ohio, had a greater population than Cincinnati. But Cincinnati had a significantly larger metropolitan-area population and was thus the larger of the two markets. Similarly, San Diego is California's second-largest city, but San Francisco is the center of a substantially larger metropolitan area and is really the "bigger town." Being associated with a big town is important to many people. Some just like the feel of it. Some may need a big city to make them feel bigger. And sometimes bigness is a measure of the urban amenities an area is likely to offer.

But bigness is not necessarily a measure of job availability in your field of interest. The fact that California is the nation's most populous state doesn't necessarily mean that you're more likely to find the job you want there than in Montana. If you operate snow-removal equipment, for example, your resume may not arouse fervid interest in the offices of the Los Angeles Street Maintenance Bureau, but you could be just the person they're looking for in Cutbank, Montana. Even assuming a person with your job title was being desperately sought in Los Angeles (perhaps to clean up after fake blizzards on the lot at Paramount), you might not want to move there. Some people just flat out don't like Los Angeles. That's an important consideration. As I said, it's not only what you want to do but where you want to do it. I've mentioned some population trends and projections, along with some job-availability information about various fields and various places, only to provide an overview that some might find useful if considering a move. I realize that the fact hundreds of thousands of jobs may be opening up in the West is of no value to a New Jersey woman who has no intention of moving. And there may be no reason for her to move. After all, she is looking for one job, not one hundred thousand. If she goes about her job search properly, chances are she can stay put.

That's where a lot of Americans seem to want to stay these days: put. More and more people have been turning down jobs when it would mean relocating. I recently read an essay on the subject by political columnist Richard Reeves:

"Census Bureau statistics have not quite caught up with the new American immobility. The latest official mobility figures indicate that 17.7 percent of adult Americans changed their address during 1976. That number was only a little lower than the annual rate of about 20 percent that has been the norm since World War II. But that slight drop . . . does indicate that people stopped moving quite as much even before high mortgage interest rates made it a significant—sometimes impossible—financial sacrifice for many people to sell old homes and buy new ones. New attitudes toward work—the 'quality of life' syndrome—certainly had something to do with all of this, but they don't explain what appears to be a much more substantial decline in mobility and what may be new patterns in American life."

The real explanation?

"Women working," Reeves said. "Two people, and often two careers, are increasingly involved in decisions that used to be made between a man and his ambition. It's another indication that the women's movement may have been the most important social development in postwar America, more important even than the impact of the GI Bill of Rights or the civil rights movement."[9]

The figures in Reeves's column were drawn from a *Business Week* report that I happened to have read earlier in my research for this chapter. Evidence of America's new immobility may be surprising, the report said, in light of many stories about the migration from the Frostbelt to the Sunbelt in the 1970s. But while the migration involved several million people—more than enough to fill the city of Chicago—they made up less than 2 percent of the U.S. population. And the number of people moving to the Sunbelt was dropping off.

Business Week used a Seattle couple as a case study in resistance to relocation:

"Robert B. Frost is one American who will not be relocating this summer despite an enticing opportunity. Avionics manager of Boeing Company's Military Airplane Division in Seattle, Frost was courted by a Los Angeles aerospace company that offered him a 30 percent raise, $25,000 to ease him into a new house and a moorage for his sailboat. But Frost, 42, decided that the offer paled beside his 7¾-percent mortgage in Seattle, his wife's nursing job and the more pleasant sailing on Puget Sound. 'The incentives companies are offering to move just aren't enough to offset things like that,' he says."[10]

The report offered other examples of workers who wouldn't budge. One company in New England was getting twice as many turndowns as it had a few years earlier from employees who were asked to move. A company moving from Portland, Oregon, to Atlanta, Georgia, hoped to get four hundred executives and professionals to join in the relocation—and got only about two hundred and fifty, even though employees were given three years to prepare for the move. The remaining one hundred fifty preferred losing jobs to leaving the area.

"The most dramatic switch," the *Business Week* article said, "has come at International Business Machines Corporation, where frequent moves have been so ingrained in the [corporate] culture that wags claim the company's initials stand for 'I've

Been Moved.' Prodded by both the national atmosphere of employee resistance and corporate doubts about the efficiency of map-hopping, IBM is cutting the percentage of its 200,000-person work force that it moves each year to less than 3 percent, from 5 percent in the mid-1970s.''

The article said the immovable employee has become a source of concern to some in business:

"A number of management experts fear that employees who are allowed to put down roots in a community will lose a sense of corporate identity, loyalty and job worth. They argue that creating a feeling of 'corporate community' by tearing down geographical ties has been a major motive—albeit an unconscious one in most cases—for the musical-chairs moving policies of [some] companies. . . . Finding substitute ways of strengthening the corporate culture will be crucial in a less mobile America. [The author of one study] is pushing a variant of the honors that Japanese companies often bestow on valued senior workers. U.S. companies, he says, should create 'senior advisory' slots to reward and motivate managers whose geographical ties make further promotions difficult.''

But what has become a problem for management could become an opening for you if you're out of work—and can handle the hassle of moving periodically. A "willing to relocate" entry on your resume could invite special attention from an employer whose people keep telling him, "Hell no, we won't go."

Finding people harder to move, some companies are moving themselves, or setting up branch offices and factories in areas with ready labor pools. Many of these facilities are being established in nonurban areas. At least two factors are at play in this development. First, some smaller cities and towns feel a need to strengthen their economic bases and are prepared to create conditions inviting to new business. Second, as we have seen, the smaller but still significant number of mobile Americans are more likely to settle in small towns than in urban centers.

The establishment or relocation of business in the boonies is not welcome news for many U.S. cities whose large minority populations already are finding work hard to come by. It is good news, on the other hand, for smaller towns with growth ambitions. And it could present opportunities for you if you're an out-of-work or unhappily employed urban dweller and wouldn't mind moving out of the city, particularly if you wouldn't mind moving to the West or South. While most of the jobs at new plants and offices in smaller cities and towns may be filled with local labor, you may have experience and skills that would be much in demand at a new business with a largely untrained work force.

If you're thinking of making such a move, take a few tips from experts on the subject. The first one is obvious: You should find out everything you can not only about the job you would be doing but also about the place where you would be living. "Do your homework first," was the way psychologist Richard Raymond put it in an article about things to do if you're relocating. Some further advice:

> Once the decision has been made to relocate, concentrate on the positive aspects of the move. Children are especially prone to picking up a parent's negative reaction to a transfer, experts warn.
>
> If a couple or a family must be separated for a while, make an extra effort to keep lines of communication open. "This is one of the most stressful times," Raymond cautioned. "There's anxiety and a feeling of being unsettled."
>
> Don't give up. Feelings of loneliness, depression and loss of control are just as much a part of relocation as excitement and a sense of adventure are. . . .
>
> Avoid the White House Syndrome, sometimes exhibited by families who relocate often. "They paint their houses only white, beige or pastel colors," Raymond said. "They do things to the house to make it easily marketable. They never really do anything that invests themselves in the house. People need to have a commitment to making a house a home."
>
> Finally, be patient. Studies indicate that complete readjustment takes about a year under the best of circumstances.[11]

In the same issue in which *Money* magazine gave us a rundown on some of the country's more inviting small cities, it carried a report on people who had moved to such places, most from larger cities. These were not people who had been fired or laid off. Most of them just seemed to want to get away. For present purposes, however, why they moved is less important than how they made out. And they seemed to be making out just fine. For example:

"Herb Mueller sought out a small city. Mueller . . . was a banker in the Los Angeles area when he and his family drove north to vacation in Oregon in 1971. He thought they'd stop in Redding, California (pop. 85,000), for gas and a bite to eat. Once he saw the place, he didn't want to leave."

Upshot: Mueller quit a fine job, moved his family to Redding and opened his own bank there.

"Now he and his wife, Carol, do just what they dreamed of doing in their off hours: loll on Lake Shasta waiting for the bass to bite by day, and lie atop their houseboat watching meteor showers at night. 'It's like being on vacation year round,' he says."[12]

Some other responses from relocaters interviewed for the *Money* article:

Patricia Sawrey, who moved with her husband and daughter from Los Angeles to Reno, Nevada: "The houses [in Reno] are affordable for young couples, it's a better place to raise children, crime is low and the lifestyle is very easy and open."

Liz Cooper, whose accountant husband moved from Philadelphia to Nashua, New Hampshire: "Russ is just as challenged as he was in Philadelphia, but he doesn't feel he's under the kind of pressure he was before."

Michael Wyant, a management consultant and developer who moved his family from Los Angeles to Redding and found he could still run his business: "With all the new technology and communications available to me, I've been able to do investment analyses of over $500 million worth of projects in ten states."

James Houlik, who moved from New York to Winston-Salem, North Carolina, to pursue a career as a performing saxophonist and found he was at most only a plane ride away from wherever he might be booked for a performance: "I think I've helped destroy the myth that you have to be in New York or Los Angeles to make it happen."

Robert Mulready, who left the Northeast and became city administrator in Davenport, Iowa: "In the big city you're just one of the also-rans. Here people want to get to know you. They care."

Judy Blinn, who found a home with a picture-window view of Mount Rainier after she and her husband quit their jobs in the Bay Area of Northern California to move to Olympia, Washington: "It would take an impossible, once-in-a-lifetime opportunity to make us even consider leaving this place."

On the other hand:

Marshall Hood, who took a newspaper job in Davenport but found he had to go to Des Moines or Chicago to do some of his shopping: "Nobody here has all-cotton Oxford shirts!"

Ron Sustana, an executive who had lived in Chicago and Los Angeles before moving to North Carolina: "You won't find a five-star French restaurant in Winston-Salem."

Althea Simmons of Washington, D.C., whose work as a director of the National Association for the Advancement of Colored People led her to conclude that blacks are likely to have job and housing problems in smaller urban areas: "They are at a disadvantage because they don't have any contacts in these small cities."

Michael Dewing, who returned to Minneapolis from Janesville, Wisconsin, after his divorce: "I didn't feel comfortable being single in a small city. Most activities there revolve around the family."

Barbara Hammerman Brody, who went through a divorce after moving from Chicago to Davenport: "In a large city, single mothers are common. Here, when you are suddenly divorced, you have a disease, and the cure is marriage."

This of course is not a scientific study. No one knows for sure what percent of people are really happy after moving from big to small cities. But "for a growing number of Americans," the *Money* report said, "the decision to leave big cities and their suburbs is becoming easier. Armed with a list of urban grievances —unsafe streets, overcrowded schools, uptight people and endless traffic—they are finding a haven in smaller cities."

But let's hear a word on behalf of a big town. In September 1977, Zenith Radio Corporation moved much of its television production overseas and shut down four plants in the Chicago area, laying off 1,500 workers. In 1980, *Forbes* magazine spent nearly two months tracking down and interviewing some 10 percent of the laid-off workers to see what had happened to them.

"None of the 150 people *Forbes* spoke to thought about leaving the Chicago area for jobs elsewhere," the magazine reported. "American workers, unlike a good many Europeans, don't seem to be inclined to follow jobs across the continent, according to First National Bank of Chicago economist Nina Klarich. 'One of the great fiascoes of the 1960s was an attempt to staff the Montana coal mines with Appalachian miners,' she says. 'These individuals clearly preferred to stay in their home communities and collect unemployment rather than move to a "foreign" area.' "[13]

Some of those thrown out of work by the Zenith shutdown in Chicago collected unemployment, too. But by the time *Forbes* got to them, 70 percent of those interviewed had found new jobs. And they hadn't found them in Davenport or Olympia or Redding. They stuck with the big town, and some did quite well. *Forbes* examined the case of Fred Wilkoszewski, who had been a maintenance chief for Zenith.

Wilkoszewski had been worried for months before the layoff. There had been rumors that operations would be moved to Taiwan and other overseas precincts. Wilkoszewski came to hate getting up in the morning. Then, one morning, he didn't have to get up. The layoff rumors were true.

"Wilkoszewski . . . was asked whether he wanted to stay on as a janitor," the *Forbes* story reported. "It meant a loss of seniority and, far worse, a cut in pay from $1,200 a month to $500. It wasn't much of a choice for a man with a wife and three small kids: either a huge pay cut or no job at all. Wilkoszewski, who years earlier had quit the construction business for Zenith 'because it was regular work, not seasonal,' became a janitor. A couple of weeks later, he took sick leave with an ulcer. He never returned to Zenith. The more than $7,000 in profitsharing he took with him somewhat eased the pain. . . . Today he works as a scaler at United Packing Company, earning about $20,000, nearly twice what he made at Zenith. And no more ulcer."

Joe Gonzalez had worked at Zenith about twenty years. Zenith offered him a different job at lower pay after the layoff. But with unemployment compensation and other benefits, plus his wife's salary and $30,000 he received in profitsharing, he was not desperate enough to accept the offer.

With nothing to do, however, Gonzales eventually got antsy. Then, almost a year after the layoff, the state employment office offered to enroll him in a twelve-week truck-driving course. His tuition would be covered under the federal Comprehensive Employment and Training Act.

"He jumped at it," *Forbes* said. "One week after he finished the course, he landed a job as a Chicago Transit Authority (CTA) bus driver, earning $11 an hour, twice what he was making at Zenith. . . . 'For the first time in two years I've got a little confidence,' he says, smiling and jauntily adjusting his cap in the rearview mirror of his bus. 'I doubt if they can send the CTA to Korea or Taiwan.' "

It was a lucky break for Joe Gonzalez when the employment office found a place for him in the truck-driving course. And it could well be that luck will figure to some extent in the direction of your career. You've probably heard at least one good-luck story about somebody who happened to be in the right place at the right time, and at least one bad-luck story about somebody who was ideally qualified for a job opening—and found out about it a day late.

Branch Rickey, the distinguished baseball executive, used to say that luck "is the residue of hard work." That may be the case often, perhaps even most of the time. But not always. I found some exceptions to the rule in a *Fortune* magazine essay quoted earlier in this chapter. The essay began with a reference to a *New York Times* story about how Army Major Stanley Daugherty was undone by a rotten piece of luck:

"He was marching his two-hundred-member company past the tent of the major general in command of Fort Riley, Kansas. The men were chanting a marching cadence that closes with the words, 'We like it here!' Unfortunately for Major Daugherty, a few of the men elected to supplement the approved text with what the *Times* cautiously characterized as 'a barnyard epithet.' After the general heard this word, the major was relieved of his command and shipped off to Fort Bragg. Another officer . . . observed sympathetically: 'It was the wrong word at the wrong place at the wrong time. Now fourteen years of work is totally destroyed for that one word.' "[14]

But the essay was largely a collection of good-luck stories, including one about a businessman who "might never have put together one of the largest companies in the U.S." if it hadn't been for "a chance encounter on a train." The man was Nate Cummings, who, we learn later on in the essay, had "put together Consolidated Foods, now No. 62 among the Fortune 500 largest industrials (1980 sales: $5.3 billion)."

"A possibly decisive event in the creation of the company was a chance meeting forty years ago, in a railroad dining car, between Cummings and Henry Crown," the story said. "Cummings was taking the train to Chicago from Baltimore, where he lived and owned a small food-wholesaling company. He was going to Chicago to try to acquire a much larger food company, Sprague Warner & Company, for which there were other bidders. Crown . . . ran the Chicago-based Material Service Corporation and was already a powerful presence in the Chicago business world. When the two men began chatting, it turned out that Crown was close to Colonel Sprague, the founder of Sprague Warner. Upon arriving in Chicago, Crown sold Sprague on Cummings, Sprague sold the other stockholders, and the deal went through.

"In its wake Cummings had a much larger base for the wave of acquisitions that snowballed into Consolidated Foods. Asked recently whether the company would exist if he hadn't met Crown on the train, Cummings replied: 'My dear fellow, I wish I could answer that. It's damned interesting.' "

The author of the essay, Daniel Seligman, also told a story about his own career:

"Three decades ago, I was an extremely junior person on a widely unread magazine, earning $69.50 per week after three and one-half years on the staff. No amount of inflation-adjusting is going to convert that figure into a decent salary. I asked for a raise to $100, quit when I was unsympathetically turned down, and was then miraculously hired when I applied for a position on *Fortune,* a widely read magazine. I have been haunted for years by the thought that I might have got that raise, or at least a little sympathy."

Seligman cited a 1972 book called *Inequality,* in which Harvard sociologist Christopher Jencks and a team of collaborators concluded that luck "has at least as much effect as competence on income."

The book was criticized, Seligman said, on the ground that Jencks and company "hadn't done a thorough enough job of measuring the personal attributes that affect income."

In a later book, *Who Gets Ahead?,* Jencks and a different group of collaborators seemed to acknowledge that the criticism had at least some merit.

"The revised finding," Seligman said, "is that men's personal characteristics at the time they enter the labor force might explain as much as half the variance in annual earnings and two-thirds of the variance in occupational status.

"[But] the still-substantial unexplained variance is more or less synonymous with luck."

Of which, I hope, you will have an abundance of the good kind.

1. Mary Tuthill, "Where the Jobs Are," *Nation's Business,* September 1980.

2. Marlys Harris, with Lani Luciano, reporter associate, "Young Americans: Careers for the Next Frontier," *Money,* June 1981.

3. "Job Horizons for Women," *Glamour,* November 1981. From *What Women Earn,* by Thelma Kandel (New York: Simon and Schuster, 1981).

4. Daniel Seligman, with Andrew C. Brown, research associate, "Success: Luck and Careers," *Fortune,* November 16, 1981.

5. John Merwin, "Have Lectures, Will Travel," *Forbes,* October 26, 1981.

6. Debra Morgenstern, "Where to Learn a Trade," *McCall's Monthly Newsletter for Women,* June 1980.

7. Carrie Tuhy, "Big Futures in Small Cities: Communities Under 250,000 Are Offering Rich Opportunities," *Money,* October 1980.

8. Patricia A. Dreyfus, "Big Futures in Small Cities: The Winning Ways of 10 That Work," *Money,* October 1980.

9. Richard Reeves, "The New Immobility: America Says Goodbye to the Moving Van," *Los Angeles Herald Examiner,* October 26, 1981.

10. "America's New Immobile Society," *Business Week,* July 27, 1981.

11. Newhouse News Service, "Psychologists Offer Tips to Ease Relocation Pains," *Los Angeles Times,* June 18, 1981.

12. Candace E. Trunzo. "Big Futures in Small Cities: Where the Living is Easy," *Money,* October 1980.

13. Bob Tamarkin, with Lisa Gross, "Starting Over in Chicago," *Forbes,* April 28, 1980.

14. Daniel Seligman, with Andrew C. Brown, research associate, "Success: Luck and Careers."

9 / *Summing Up*

LEARNING TO FORGET

Walking into a theater one evening, you pass an attractive older couple. You stop, take another step, then stop again, shaken, as if you had just viewed an apparition. The movie you were going to see has suddenly lost its appeal. You walk out.

You do not know the older couple. You had never even seen them before this evening. But the man looked familiar. He looked like your father, who died a month ago.

The man of course did not intend to ruin your evening. Sheer accident brought the two of you to the same place at the same time. Life is full of such accidents, full of unintended reminders of unpleasant events.

A person just rejected by a spouse or lover may find an evening in ruins after seeing a young couple walking hand in hand. It's a perfectly common, innocent scene. But it can be painful for someone who no longer has a hand to hold.

Or suppose you've been fired. You may pick up a book and come across a character with a job like the one you lost. You'll probably have to put the book down a moment, until that familiar uneasy feeling passes. On television, you may be watching a situation comedy in which the blunder-prone lead character has lost his glasses, can't read anything smaller than a billboard and is fired after inadvertently setting off a panic by walking into the women's restroom. The humor of the situation (such as it is) escapes you. If you should happen to be an ex-football coach, you might be watching TV when a game comes on and a coach is seen leading his players onto the field. Once again, that old, uneasy feeling. You no longer have a team.

These reminders are of course unintentional, not conspiratorial. The rest of the world has not plotted to keep unhappy experiences fixed in your mind.

But people won't let you forget if you've ever been fired. Quite without design, in the course of their ordinary affairs, they'll keep sending you reminders of the sort given the man entering the theater.

So if you can't keep that job loss entirely out of mind, don't worry. Being reminded occasionally of a firing is as normal as being reminded of the death of someone close to you. It's not the sort of thing you should be expected to forget.

But, to repeat a warning given earlier, you must set up a defense system to protect yourself from overexposure to negative incoming signals. You can't let them consume you. That's one of several points I want to repeat for emphasis in this final chapter.

If you've been fired and can't stop thinking about it, you may sense you have a real fight on your hands. In fact, the fight is not on your hands but in your head. You're struggling for control of your own mind.

If you want to win that fight—and, for sanity's sake, you had better—try looking at your situation this way: You have a choice of pointing yourself in either of two directions, backward or forward. The human inclination, after a personal tragedy, is not to look forward. The tendency is rather to let the mind function as a sort of videorecorder and keep replaying events of the tragedy. In your case, there will probably be a slow-motion replay, repeated several times, when you get to the scene where the boss calls you in and says, "I'm afraid I have some rather unpleasant news." Then the tape will run on, reminding you of the many humiliations that followed the firing.

I've read that some experts on the human mind think a little indulgence in grief is a good thing. Your memory keeps reminding you of a tragedy until your emotions are spent and you finally come to accept it as a fact. Or something like that. But personal experience tells me that you can overindulge. You can almost devour yourself.

Happily, experience also has shown that the problem is beatable, or at least treatable. I've saved one of my favorite illustrations for now. It was provided by Pete McCulley, who lost his job as head coach of the San Francisco 49ers in the middle of the 1978 season. The first word came from a sportswriter who called at midnight, asking McCulley to respond to a report that he was being released. McCulley told the writer it was just a rumor and went back to bed.

McCulley told me the rest of the story in a letter:

"However, the next day was Halloween, and when I drove to work at 4:30 a.m. a black cat crossed my path from left to right. Although I had never been a superstitious person, I became anxious. . . .

"The rumor was confirmed in the office of the general manager, Joe Thomas, at mid-morning, October 31, 1978. I cannot say that I was totally surprised because I had not been surprised by anything since I found out that ice cream cones were not filled all the way to the bottom. I told Joe that he was making an error because we were basically an expansion team and actually playing over our heads in losing close games. History proved this to be a true statement.

"Attaining my career dream of being a head coach of a National Football League team and then being released for not producing a quick winner was a crushing blow to my spirit. Frankly, during the three months between jobs, I wasted time being miserable and sucking my thumb. As a coach, I had experienced numerous victories over every kind of defeat and difficulty. . . . Ordinarily, when I had fallen in a mud hole, I checked my hip pocket to see if I had caught a fish.

"However, in this case I needed a good dose of positive thinking to provide fuel to flame the hungry kind of feeling that had always burned deep inside of me to attain goals and to be a winner."

McCulley caught on as an assistant coach with the New York Jets in 1979. Two years later, he was still troubled that he had been unable "to overcome a career setback" by getting another head coaching job.

"[But] from a personal standpoint," he said, "I have been able to recover from a wounded spirit. In this instance, Dr. Norman Vincent Peale's practical approach to Christian living was precisely what I needed for full recovery and peace of mind. The New York move provided the opportunity for me to become a member of the Marble Collegiate Church in Manhattan, where Dr. Peale is pastor."

As sales of Dr. Peale's books attest, his brand of positive thinking has wide appeal. If it doesn't quite fit your needs, find another brand. Or manufacture your own. One way or another, you need to learn to think positively.

When McCulley said he "wasted time being miserable and sucking my thumb," he was talking about time spent thinking back to his sacking in San Francisco. As he discovered, back is the wrong way to look. The past can't make you happy, even if it was a largely pleasant past. The only days you have to live are ahead of you, not behind you. If you go through the rest of your life looking in the rearview mirror, you may miss some good things up ahead, and run into a few bad ones you might have evaded by watching where you were going instead of where you'd been.

Nearly everything your mind is exposed to affects how you feel. It's difficult to filter out everything that might depress you. And there is of course some negative information you can't ignore. If someone told me, "Hey, George, your car was just stolen and I think I know who took it," it would perhaps be imprudent of me to say, "I don't want to hear about it. Things like that depress me." But you can shield yourself from a lot of unnecessary negative thought. One way is to avoid spending a lot of time with negative people. And you can limit the amount of time you spend grappling with negative thoughts that are bound to occur to you spontaneously. For example, thoughts about that job you lost.

One approach, as I suggested earlier, is to imagine yourself switching your mind to a different channel, as you would a TV set. Any time a depressing thought about a past failure occurs to you, and dwelling on it will solve no present problem, tune it out and tune in a positive thought. Or think of yourself as a coach. Your mind is the field of play, and the thoughts running around in there are your players. A negative thought is a player who is messing up, hurting the team. If you spot such a player, make an immediate substitution. Send in a positive thought.

Getting rid of negative thoughts may be hard work at first. If you're alone when one comes along, it may help to seek assistance. Get on the phone, or find someone in the family to talk to, and strike up a conversation about something positive. The technique is hardly new. You've doubtless heard people cut short pointlessly depressing discussions by saying, "If you don't mind, I'd like to change the subject." That's what you should tell yourself when your brain tries to lock in on a useless negative thought. It takes practice, but it works.

This doesn't mean you'll never again be bothered by a negative thought. You may remember back in Chapter One I conceded it was probably a mistake when I turned down the new contract the Redskins offered me after the 1977 season. When I wrote that, I was thinking a negative thought. But I did not allow myself to dwell on it. That's an important difference. It's the difference between recognizing a mistake and wallowing in regret over it.

If we don't recognize our mistakes, we'll probably repeat them. So when you foul up, admit it. Learn from it. That's using a negative thought for a positive purpose. But once it has served that purpose, get rid of it. *Don't dwell on it.* That's my approach when I think about leaving the Redskins. I just won't let myself waste time wondering how things might have been. It's much more important to plan how things are going to be.

HOW YOU SEE YOURSELF

Positive thoughts are not just useful as depression fighters. They're always useful. Much of the time, your mind is probably more or less in neutral. You're neither particularly high nor particularly low. You can keep yourself higher oftener if you make latching onto positive thoughts a matter of routine.

I used to tell my players they should picture themselves making a big play—catching a touchdown pass, throwing a great block, recovering an opponent's fumble, blocking a kick or making an interception. The idea was to make that big play a goal. Because big plays are what winning teams are made of, the goal would look so desirable that the players would be willing to work hard to achieve it. The hard work was what really carried them to their objective, of course, but seeing the goal made the work look worthwhile and motivated them to get it done.

I don't believe the saying that wishing can't make it so. Not entirely, anyway. Wishing you could do something may lead to thinking you could do it and then to knowing you can. By the time you get to that third step, you've developed a positive self-image. Most of my top players—Deacon Jones, Billy Kilmer, Diron Talbert, Kenny Houston, Bob Brunet, Ron McDole, Roman Gabriel, Mark Moseley and others—developed that sort of image. Most unsuccessful people I've known have not. The lesson is that positive thought breeds positive action. Negative thought breeds failure.

I believe some teams in the National Football League lose year after year because they have an agenda for losing. They may not want to lose, but they seem to expect to. If they don't find it desirable, they seem to find it tolerable. They've simply got the wrong attitude. A club executive or coach whose team has just gone 4-and-12 may be dismayed when he looks at next year's schedule and discovers his team is opening against the Dallas Cowboys. He'd just as soon not start with a loss.

In fact, a game against a great team like Dallas should be seen not as an ordeal but as an opportunity. Because only that recognition will give the coach, the players and the rest of the organization the kind of encouragement they need to get ready for the game.

In my first years in Los Angeles, I used to say that to beat the Green Bay Packers I first had to defeat my front office, my coaches and my players. If I could do that, we would then be ready for the Packers. What I meant was that the organization had to defeat its negative instincts. It had to start thinking of a victory over Green Bay not as something that might happen if we got lucky, but as something that *would* happen if we got ready.

I'm not suggesting you can positive-think yourself into ten consecutive perfect seasons. We didn't win all our games with Green Bay even after we developed a more positive outlook. But you'll be a winner more often if you keep telling yourself that's what you're going to be. Because, in telling yourself that, you'll also be telling yourself to work harder.

These rules, I think, are not just for football teams. They apply with equal force in other fields. Developing a positive self-image not only makes it easier for a person to land a job but to land promotions later.

Most people can start to improve their self-images just by making an inventory of the positive things they have going for them. Take good health. If you've got that, you're already ahead of a lot of ulcerous millionaires. If you've also got a good family, and good friends, you're really up to your eyebrows in assets. Even if you're out of work, your inventory may show that the positives in your life outnumber the negatives two to one. As I suggested earlier, one good way to get a reading on how well off you are is to spend some of your spare time doing volunteer work for the hospitalized, the handicapped and others who are really having a hard time.

If your health is good, treat it as you would a good job: Make sure you don't lose it. One way to do that, as already suggested, is to exercise. Work out every day if you can. You don't have to run ten miles. You don't have to run at all if it does nothing for you. Get a bicycle or choose another form of exercise, even walking. But keep your body in tune. It's amazing how you can improve yourself mentally by improving yourself physically. I've never had a workout that didn't leave me elated. I once wrote this little essay about it:

> A workout is 25% PERSPIRATION and 75% DETERMINATION. Stated another way, it is one part physical exertion and three parts self-discipline. Doing it is easy once you get started.
>
> A workout makes you better today than you were yesterday. It strengthens the body, relaxes the mind, toughens the spirit. When you work out regularly, your problems diminish and your confidence grows.
>
> A workout is a personal triumph over laziness and procrastination. It is the badge of a WINNER, the mark of an organized, goal-oriented person who has taken charge of his or her destiny.
>
> A workout is a wise use of time and an INVESTMENT in excellence. It is a way of preparing for life's challenges and proving to yourself that you have what it takes to do what is necessary.
>
> A workout is a key that helps unlock the door to OPPORTUNITY and SUCCESS. Hidden within each of us is an extraordinary force. Physical and mental fitness are the triggers that can release it.
>
> A workout is a form of REBIRTH. When you finish a good workout, you don't simply feel better. YOU FEEL BETTER ABOUT YOURSELF.

One time I was assigned by CBS to do an NFL game in Buffalo. I like to get in a daily workout when I'm on the road, but it was late November and the forecast in Buffalo was for less than ideal workout weather. So I decided to get up early Saturday morning and work out before leaving Los Angeles. As it developed, the weather at home was no jogger's dream, either. It was raining when the alarm rang at 5 a.m., and I hadn't slept well. Right there I had two excuses for calling off the workout. I managed to talk myself into my jogging clothes and put on a waterproof jacket and a hat, but I still wasn't enthusiastic about my predawn mission.

I became even less so when I got outside. The first quarter mile of my running course is uphill, and fighting that grade at 5:15 a.m. would be bad enough even on a dry surface. I thought of turning around and going home.

I was soon glad I didn't. For one thing, no one was out. There wasn't a car in sight. Well, I thought, at least I won't have to worry about traffic. I was starting to get warmed up now and having the outdoors all to myself was so exhilarating that I started singing "Oh, What a Beautiful Morning!" and laughing to myself. The rain felt great. But what felt even greater was the realization that I had enough self-discipline to push myself into the workout. If I had stayed in bed, I really would have missed something.

I don't want to make it sound as though thinking positive thoughts and working out every day will cure all your problems if you don't have a job. Work is often the cement that holds our lives together. It fixes our hours and many of our relationships. It structures our days. It keeps us from becoming disorganized. It gives us a sense of accomplishment. Even if we didn't need it to buy the necessities of life, work would be important. But developing a positive attitude, learning to improve your self-image and keeping in good shape will make you a more attractive job candidate, and a happier person once you're on the job again.

KEEP BUSY

A person who sits around, waiting for a job offer to fall through the transom, is not just killing time; he is killing opportunities. He is also leaving himself especially vulnerable to those destructive negative thoughts we were just talking about. Force yourself out of bed. Force yourself out of the house. Force yourself to stay in the hunt until you're a former unemployed person.

One way to prod yourself into keeping busy is to keep a daily record of your activities. You can account for an entire day on one sheet of paper. If that sheet has little or nothing on it when you go to bed, you'll know you've accomplished little or nothing that day. I think this is a really effective tool for keeping after yourself.

I made up a form of my own to use in keeping a daily record. See the sample that follows.

[Date]

Job Contact_____	Today's Accomplishments
Company_____	_____
Address_____	_____
Phone_____	_____
Interview Time_____	_____
	_____
	_____
_____	_____
	_____
Job Contact_____	_____
Company_____	_____
Address_____	Tomorrow's Priorities
Phone_____	_____
Interview Time_____	_____
	_____
_____	_____
	_____
Job Contact_____	_____
Company_____	_____
Address_____	_____
Phone_____	_____
Interview Time_____	_____

You can produce multiple copies of a homemade form by using carbon paper or (if one is available) a photocopier. Or you can forget about making up a form and just buy an inexpensive tablet, reserving one page for each day's entries.

On my form, you'll notice, there are spaces for recording three job contacts a day. That doesn't mean I never went to bed until

I had made my third contact of the day. Some days I didn't make any. The spaces are there just in case they're needed. The same goes for the spaces reserved for "Today's Accomplishments" and "Tomorrow's Priorities." I've left room for ten brief entries under each category. That doesn't mean you'll turn into a frog at midnight if you haven't accomplished exactly ten things since breakfast, or that your hair will all come out before morning if you haven't listed precisely ten priorities for tomorrow. But if you go to bed leaving an almost empty page, you'll know you've had an almost empty day.

One way to help keep yourself occupied is to take a part-time job. If it looks as if you're going to be in an extended holding pattern before you find the job you really want, start looking for a full-time job outside your area of primary interest. In other words, don't wait for that ideal job too long. For one thing, there's no guarantee your dream ship will ever come in. For another, you're more likely to get job offers when you're already working. ("If this person is a desirable applicant," a prospective employer may say, "how come he's unemployed?") As a general rule, long periods of unemployment don't look good on a resume. If that ideal job does come along, you may look like a more attractive prospect if you're working than if you aren't.

After the Rams and I parted company the last time, I did many job interviews but passed up many offers. I eventually went to work for CBS as an analyst on NFL broadcasts—and enjoyed it —but I could have had a full-time position if I'd wanted one. Looking back, I suspect I should have taken one. I rejected some interesting offers.

If you have to get back to work to keep body and soul united, be as choosy as your situation permits. The fact there are no openings in your preferred field doesn't necessarily mean you have to take the first job that comes along. Even if you're in a financial bind, you can probably spend at least a week or two surveying the field without risking starvation.

I think it's important to avoid being impetuous. Otherwise, you may wind up on a job you simply can't live with. If that happens, you'll probably quit before long. Then you'll have to explain to your next prospective employer why you left so soon. Even if you had a good reason, the experience may raise a question about your judgment: Why didn't you give the job a closer look before taking it?

HOW MUCH IS ENOUGH?

Money should of course be an important consideration in your analysis of a job offer. Some of the best things in life may be free, but a decent place to live, for example, is not among them. Also, most nutritionists recommend that we have at least an occasional meal. For that, you may have observed, there is a charge.

Still, the importance of money can be overestimated. While probably all of us would be unhappy if reduced below a certain level of comfort (the amount varying according to taste and experience), I've known people with $10 million who seemed no happier than some others who might have trouble raising $10,000. After you've reached the point where you can live comfortably, a law of diminishing returns may set in. That point, of course, is not the same for everyone. A bank chairman's son or daughter, having become accustomed to butlers and Bentleys, would perhaps never be satisfied with a standard of living that might seem quite adequate to the son or daughter of a bank teller. But how much fun you're getting out of a job or business may be more important than how much money you get out of it. I once turned down a job I was told could have brought me about $1 million a year.

To be sure, many wealthy people are in the dollar chase not to acquire more creature comforts but to accumulate more power. If your ambition is to become one of the nation's top movers and shakers, you'll probably need a fortune to pull it off. But some people seem to chase money without really knowing why. A writer once put it this way:

A phantom only, man goes his
  ways;
  like vapor only are his
    restless pursuits;
  he heaps up stores and knows
    not who will use them.[1]

SMELL THE FLOWERS

Years ago, when I was coaching the Rams, I wrote: "To me, leisure time consists of the five or six hours each night when one is asleep. The human body was designed to be completely regenerated on a few hours of good, sound sleep. Waking hours tend to be wasted when put to leisure purposes."

Now I'm not so sure. Being out of work gives you an opportunity to get to know yourself better. You have more time to try things you could never get around to when you were working every day. One thing I discovered is that leisure time really can be fulfilling. I didn't have time to take in the scenery, let alone to stop and smell the flowers, when I was going sixty miles an hour sixteen or eighteen hours a day.

I got some good advice from Tommy Prothro, who had been coach of the Rams before my last tour of duty in Los Angeles (and who, like me, had been fired by Carroll Rosenbloom). Tommy told me how much he and his wife, Shirley, enjoyed traveling after he lost the Ram job. I got another good tip from Virginia Madden, whose husband, John, coached the Oakland Raiders before becoming a television star on Lite beer commercials. "There is more to life," she told me, "than just football."

So I decided to look at the other side. Etty and I began traveling, usually taking at least one other member of the family along. We went to Athens, Paris, Cannes, Rome, Naples, Capri, Tokyo, Hong Kong, Cabo San Lucas, even to the Northern Slopes of Alaska. Virginia Madden was right: The world is more than one hundred yards long.

That kind of travel is expensive. But I had been well paid. And I owed it to Etty and the family. When I was coaching I rarely took a vacation of more than ten days because I thought I had to get back to work.

What I'm leading up to is that the postfiring period is a good time to do things you've always wanted to do but never got to for lack of time. I appreciate that not everyone can pack up the family and fly to Paris. But if you were on the job for some years before the axe fell, you could probably afford to spend a little time at that lake or mountain resort you always talked of visiting. If you hadn't been working that long and the bank balance is a little undernourished, maybe you could get away for just a weekend or two. If you can't get out of town, at least get out of your chair. You might try a couple of the diversions I suggested earlier: planting a garden or tackling one of those home-repair projects that have awaited your attention the last five years. Travel, gardening and puttering around the house perform a dual function. They're enjoyable, and they help keep you busy.

Until my last firing, I would have told you I could live as easily without my kidneys as I could without football. I was wrong, though I still miss the game. You can't spend twenty-nine years at something, loving every day of it (unless it happens to be a day on which you lose a game or your job), and then walk away without giving it another thought. Even after four firings, I still wanted to coach. But I made up my mind I wasn't going to be one of those hat-in-hand supplicants who would agree to run out and get the owner's coffee just to get back into coaching again. I would not go to work for just any owner. While a club owner and his organization were examining my credentials, I'd want to be going over theirs.

As a couple of my former NFL coaching colleagues indicated in an earlier chapter, most pro football owners don't like strong coaches. That may explain why I rather easily avoided being suffocated under an avalanche of offers after leaving the Rams the last time. I've thought that through, and all I can say is this: Look at my record. Then look at the records of most NFL clubs. If they don't want to hire George Allen, that's their problem.

IT'S UP TO YOU

Whether you're an athlete preparing for a game, a product rep preparing for a sales presentation—or a disemployed person preparing for a job interview—you've got a job that only you can do. Others may help you, but you can't count on them. No one else is as interested in your career as you are. Your coach or your boss or your friends may encourage you, even push you, but you've got to make the big push yourself. It's up to you to set the pace of your life. If you're out of work, you may be tempted to make the pace slow. But the time you seem least able to force yourself out of the house, for example, is the very time you must force yourself out.

I'm somehow reminded of a line from a Marx Brothers movie. (My reproduction may not be verbatim but will be close enough.) Groucho, Chico and Harpo are standing inside a railroad depot. A departing passenger, obviously running late and in desperate need of direction, rushes up to Groucho.

PASSENGER: Where's the train?

GROUCHO: Out on the track. It very seldom comes in here.

As you would not expect a train to seek you out inside a depot, you should not expect a job to seek you out at home. Few employers make house calls.

The analogy is admittedly inexact. Perhaps a better one could be found in gardening, a pursuit I've embraced in recent years. In starting a garden, of course, the first step is to plant seeds. You can never be sure which seeds will grow, no matter how faithfully you water and fertilize. But you know one thing: Your chances of growing radishes are rather slim if you plant no radish seeds.

Similarly, jobs come from planting job seeds. And, since you never know which seeds will grow, it's a good idea to plant a slew of them. When you're pretty sure you've planted more than enough, plant a few more. Keep pushing yourself. Make another phone call. Write another letter. Add another contact to your employment network.

Most successful people I've known have been tireless planters. They don't keep planting job seeds, of course, because they don't need jobs. They plant other kinds of opportunity seeds. They invest in new ideas. Like gardeners studying seed catalogs, they follow the literature of their fields, looking for even more new ideas. They never stop making contacts, because someone they meet today may be a customer or a supplier, or just a friend, tomorrow.

The development of a plant from a seed is one of nature's miracles. Planting seeds in your business and social worlds can produce results almost as miraculous. All you have to remember is not to stop. Just keep planting.

PARTING THOUGHT

This book may not get you a job overnight. But I think some of the expert advice I've passed along will be helpful. One of the most important lessons is that you've got to have a plan. Without one, you're simply adrift. You don't know where you're going. And when you arrive you may discover it's the wrong destination.

A plan is a map. You lay it out and measure how far it is from where you are to where you want to go. Then you plan the trip. When you've taken a few trips, you will discover that little details in planning are as important as the big picture. In fact, details are what big pictures are made of. If you don't give careful attention to the details, the big picture will not be suitable for framing.

I neglected to take care of a detail when the Redskins played the Miami Dolphins in the Super Bowl. I later confessed to the omission in a magazine article:

> I have a sign on my desk that says THE TEAM IS NEVER UP! I put that there after the Super Bowl. We were flat for the Super Bowl,

hard as that is to imagine. Just before the game I was going to talk to the team and rile them up. I thought the dressing room was subdued. But then I thought to myself, I don't have to do that. This is the Super Bowl. It's the biggest game of their lives.

That sign reminds me never to take anything for granted.[2]

No detail is too small if part of an important undertaking. Knowing your work in detail is knowing what you're doing. Winners attend to details; losers do not. Winners know why they win; losers don't know why they lose.

Winners also invite risks, welcome challenges. I don't mean that you should accept an invitation to join an expedition to the summit of Mount Everest with no climbing experience, or that you should invest your life savings in International Sky Hooks just to show you don't flinch from risks. I mean that if you're confident you can take on any of three jobs, don't reject the second and third just because they look harder than the first. Everything else being about equal, the most challenging of the three may well be the best of the three. The tougher the job, the greater the reward when it is accomplished. Meanwhile, of course, the tougher the fight. But that shouldn't worry you.

One thing I've learned is that you must fight all your life for everything. No matter what your position in life, no matter what you have achieved, you must keep fighting. You cannot rest on yesterday's accomplishments. It's a test that challenges your character, and a test I relish every day.

1. Ps. 39:7, "A Psalm of David," *New American Bible,* Michelangelo Edition (Chicago: The Catholic Press, 1971). *The Authorized King James Version* (Chicago: Good Counsel Publishers, 1965) assigns the verse a different number (6 instead of 7) and gives this rendering: "Surely every man walketh in a vain shew: surely they are disquieted in vain: he heapeth up riches and knoweth not who shall gather them."

2. George Allen, with Joe Marshall, "A Hundred Percent Is Not Enough," *Sports Illustrated,* July 9, 1973.

PUBLISHER'S EPILOGUE

Less than two months after this book was completed, George Allen returned (momentarily) to professional football, becoming president and chief operating manager of the Montreal Alouettes of the Canadian Football League. Under his agreement with the club owner, Allen had the right to back out if unsatisfied after reviewing the team's financial position. Upon careful analysis, Allen decided to linger no longer and, for the first time, fired his owner.

Appendix

PROJECTED 1990 EMPLOYMENT IN CIVILIAN OCCUPATIONS WITH 25,000 OR MORE WORKERS

Occupation	1978, Actual	Employment* 1990, Low Projection	1990, High Projection	% Change, 1978–90 Low	High
Total, all occupations	97,610,000	119,590,000	127,907,000	22.5	31.0
Professional, technical & related workers	15,570,000	20,038,000	21,119,000	28.7	35.6
Engineers	1,071,000	1,504,000	1,624,000	40.4	51.6
Aero-astronautic	57,000	98,000	104,000	70.3	80.9
Chemical	53,000	68,000	73,000	28.9	37.7
Civil	149,000	208,000	218,000	39.4	45.6
Electrical	291,000	441,000	479,000	51.2	64.4
Industrial	109,000	146,000	159,000	34.0	46.5
Mechanical	199,000	274,000	300,000	37.6	50.7
Life & physical scientists	236,000	299,000	316,000	26.4	33.6
Biological scientists	42,000	51,000	54,000	21.8	28.9
Chemists	90,000	113,000	120,000	24.9	32.2
Geologists	33,000	50,000	53,000	52.1	61.4

SOURCE: U.S. Department of Labor, Bureau of Labor Statistics. Adapted from table in *Monthly Labor Review,* August 1981.

* The high and low employment projections for 1990 are based on different sets of assumptions regarding productivity and other factors. In the table from which these figures were taken, the Bureau of Labor Statistics presented three projections of employment in 1990. One is omitted here. It yields figures in between those of the high and low projections.

Occupation	1978, Actual	Employment* 1990, Low Projection	1990, High Projection	% Change, 1978–90 Low	High
Engineering & science technicians	1,160,000	1,577,000	1,700,000	36.0	46.5
Drafters	293,000	412,000	446,000	40.6	52.2
Electrical & electronic technicians	319,000	464,000	512,000	45.4	60.2
Industrial engineering technicians	31,000	40,000	44,000	30.4	41.3
Mechanical engineering technicians	45,000	61,000	67,000	36.0	49.7
Surveyors	54,000	73,000	78,000	35.2	44.7
Medical workers, except technicians	2,026,000	2,928,000	3,094,000	44.6	52.8
Dentists	149,000	208,000	223,000	39.6	49.2
Dietitians	41,000	61,000	65,000	49.7	58.6
Nurses, professional	1,026,000	1,542,000	1,618,000	50.3	57.7
Optometrists	25,000	33,000	36,000	29.7	40.6
Pharmacists	140,000	159,000	171,000	13.4	22.4
Physicians, medical & osteopathic	447,000	626,000	665,000	40.0	48.7
Therapists	139,000	210,000	220,000	51.5	58.7
Physical therapists	31,000	49,000	52,000	57.6	66.5
Speech & hearing clinicians	34,000	52,000	53,000	54.5	58.3
Veterinarians	30,000	47,000	51,000	56.1	70.3
Health technologists & technicians	1,246,000	1,811,000	1,906,000	45.3	52.9
Dental assistants	123,000	193,000	198,000	57.5	60.9
Dental hygienists	53,000	84,000	86,000	57.9	61.4
Health records technologists	30,000	44,000	46,000	47.1	53.6
Licensed practical nurses	491,000	707,000	752,000	43.9	53.0
Medical technicians	82,000	119,000	127,000	46.0	55.3
Medical lab technologists	98,000	141,000	149,000	43.9	52.7
Surgical technicians	30,000	44,000	46,000	48.1	54.6
X-ray technicians	86,000	126,000	133,000	47.4	54.7

Technicians, excluding health, science & engineering	271,000	343,000	362,000	26.8	33.8
Airplane pilots	74,000	94,000	101,000	27.9	35.5
Air traffic controllers	28,000	34,000	34,000	21.7	24.2
Technical assistants, library	34,000	48,000	49,000	42.1	42.8
Computer specialists	389,000	738,000	793,000	89.8	104.0
Computer programmers	204,000	354,000	381,000	73.6	86.9
Computer systems analysts	185,000	384,000	412,000	107.7	123.0
Social scientists	176,000	243,000	256,000	38.1	45.5
Economists	27,000	41,000	43,000	54.2	62.9
Psychologists	78,000	107,000	111,000	36.8	42.7
Teachers	3,877,000	4,079,000	4,113,000	5.2	6.1
Adult education teachers	105,000	123,000	126,000	18.0	20.7
College & university teachers	618,000	557,000	560,000	−9.8	−9.3
Teachers, vocational education & training	26,000	33,000	34,000	26.5	30.3
Teachers, college	454,000	409,000	410,000	−10.1	−9.7
Graduate assistants	131,000	110,000	110,000	−16.4	−16.1
Elementary school teachers	1,277,000	1,550,000	1,556,000	21.4	21.8
Preschool & kindergarten teachers	455,000	574,000	579,000	26.2	27.3
Secondary school teachers	1,229,000	1,071,000	1,075,000	−12.9	−12.5
Selected writers, artists & entertainers	888,000	1,117,000	1,198,000	25.8	34.9
Commercial artists	100,000	122,000	134,000	22.2	34.0
Designers	169,000	194,000	212,000	15.2	25.5
Musicians, instrumental	126,000	160,000	166,000	27.1	31.7
Photographers	77,000	104,000	113,000	35.9	47.2
Public relations specialists	81,000	102,000	109,000	26.1	34.8
Radio & TV announcers	46,000	66,000	68,000	43.0	48.7
Reporters & correspondents	54,000	68,000	74,000	27.6	37.4
Sports instructors	34,000	41,000	43,000	20.2	26.6
Writers & editors	109,000	142,000	155,000	30.3	41.6

Occupation	1978, Actual	Employment* 1990, Low Projection	1990, High Projection	% Change, 1978–90 Low	High
Other professional & technical workers	4,183,000	5,338,000	5,692,000	27.6	36.1
Accountants & auditors	777,000	1,031,000	1,107,000	32.7	42.5
Appraisers, real estate	32,000	47,000	50,000	46.4	56.9
Architects	66,000	106,000	112,000	60.2	70.2
Assessors	30,000	38,000	38,000	28.0	30.3
Buyers, retail & wholesale trade	238,000	296,000	320,000	24.4	34.1
Caseworkers	236,000	338,000	350,000	43.3	48.4
Clergy	287,000	292,000	313,000	1.7	9.2
Community organization workers	49,000	71,000	74,000	46.7	51.4
Cost estimators	80,000	105,000	112,000	31.6	40.8
Directors, religious education & activities	36,000	37,000	40,000	3.3	11.1
Employment interviewers	51,000	86,000	95,000	66.6	85.5
Foresters	26,000	32,000	34,000	22.1	27.3
Law clerks	30,000	43,000	48,000	44.0	62.5
Lawyers	380,000	524,000	580,000	37.8	52.7
Paralegal personnel	28,000	66,000	75,000	132.3	165.7
Librarians	130,000	139,000	142,000	6.8	8.8
Personnel & labor-relations specialists	169,000	205,000	217,000	21.1	28.2
Purchasing agents & buyers	164,000	200,000	214,000	22.0	30.7
Recreation workers, group	121,000	152,000	160,000	26.4	32.6
Tax examiners, collectors & revenue agents	50,000	60,000	61,000	19.4	21.6
Tax preparers	29,000	47,000	54,000	64.5	87.7
Travel agents & accommodations appraisers	45,000	70,000	74,000	55.6	65.5
Underwriters	70,000	90,000	93,000	28.4	33.9
Vocational & educational counselors	202,000	212,000	215,000	4.7	6.3
Managers, officials & proprietors	8,802,000	10,484,000	11,257,000	19.1	27.9

Auto parts department managers	48,000	54,000	59,000	13.2	23.0
Auto service department managers	60,000	69,000	75,000	15.0	25.0
Construction inspectors, public administration	44,000	61,000	62,000	37.4	39.8
Inspectors, excluding construction, public administration	104,000	125,000	128,000	20.6	22.9
Postmasters & superintendents	28,000	29,000	30,000	4.1	7.9
Railroad conductors	33,000	31,000	34,000	−6.6	2.9
Restaurant, cafe & bar managers	499,000	642,000	680,000	28.6	36.2
Sales managers, retail trade	261,000	323,000	351,000	24.1	34.8
Store managers	926,000	1,102,000	1,183,000	18.9	27.8
Wholesalers	234,000	279,000	307,000	19.6	31.3
Salesworkers	6,443,000	7,989,000	8,632,000	24.0	34.0
Real estate brokers	34,000	48,000	52,000	42.3	55.9
Sales agents & representatives, real estate	255,000	394,000	430,000	54.1	68.4
Sales agents & representatives, insurance	310,000	399,000	420,000	28.6	35.7
Sales agents & representatives, security	55,000	80,000	92,000	45.8	66.8
Sales clerks	2,771,000	3,362,000	3,601,000	21.3	30.0
Clerical workers	17,820,000	22,219,000	23,705,000	24.7	33.0
Adjustment clerks	37,000	45,000	48,000	23.9	29.8
Bank tellers	440,000	601,000	619,000	36.4	40.6
New accounts tellers	48,000	65,000	67,000	34.6	39.2
Tellers	392,000	536,000	552,000	36.6	40.8
Bookkeepers & accounting clerks	1,628,000	1,982,000	2,131,000	21.8	30.9
Accounting clerks	700,000	835,000	895,000	19.3	27.8
Bookkeepers, hand	927,000	1,147,000	1,236,000	23.7	33.3
Cashiers	1,501,000	2,046,000	2,165,000	36.3	44.3
Claims adjustors	65,000	95,000	98,000	46.6	51.6
Claims clerks	63,000	92,000	96,000	47.3	52.8
Claims examiners, insurance	38,000	58,000	59,000	51.5	54.7
Clerical supervisors	402,000	518,000	552,000	29.0	37.4

Occupation	1978, Actual	Employment* 1990, Low Projection	1990, High Projection	% Change, 1978–90 Low	High
Collectors, bill & account	85,000	108,000	119,000	26.5	39.5
Credit clerks, banking & insurance	47,000	62,000	68,000	31.0	43.9
Desk clerks, except bowling floor	75,000	97,000	109,000	29.3	46.1
Dispatchers, police, fire & ambulance	46,000	60,000	61,000	28.2	30.5
Dispatchers, vehicle service or work	89,000	108,000	116,000	21.6	29.6
Eligibility workers, welfare	30,000	38,000	39,000	29.7	32.2
File clerks	251,000	328,000	349,000	30.8	39.3
General clerks, office	2,269,000	2,799,000	3,002,000	23.3	32.3
Insurance clerks, medical	63,000	93,000	97,000	46.7	53.9
Library assistants	117,000	128,000	129,000	8.8	10.0
Mail carriers, postal service	237,000	260,000	270,000	9.8	13.8
Mail clerks	75,000	94,000	99,000	25.2	31.6
Marking clerks, trade	44,000	54,000	57,000	21.2	27.9
Messengers	47,000	60,000	64,000	28.2	37.4
Meter readers, utilities	28,000	32,000	38,000	14.6	33.6
Office machine operators	842,000	1,133,000	1,211,000	34.5	43.8
Bookkeeping & billing operators	218,000	283,000	301,000	29.8	37.9
Bookkeeping, billing machine operators	166,000	212,000	228,000	27.7	37.6
Proof machine operators	44,000	60,000	61,000	37.1	39.6
Computer, peripheral equipment operators	215,000	389,000	415,000	81.3	93.2
Computer operators	169,000	317,000	338,000	87.9	100.7
Peripheral EDP equipment operators	46,000	72,000	76,000	57.3	65.5
Duplicating machine operators	31,000	38,000	41,000	22.5	31.0
Keypunch operators	295,000	316,000	341,000	7.0	15.6
Order clerks	240,000	289,000	316,000	20.2	31.5
Payroll & timekeeping clerks	172,000	211,000	226,000	22.1	31.0
Personnel clerks	90,000	111,000	118,000	23.4	30.1
Postal clerks	310,000	309,000	321,000	−0.3	3.4

Procurement clerks	39,000	46,000	50,000	19.5	28.4
Production clerks	192,000	234,000	257,000	22.3	34.0
Raters	51,000	63,000	66,000	23.6	28.7
Receptionists	369,000	505,000	540,000	37.0	46.4
Reservations agents	52,000	55,000	59,000	6.6	13.6
Secretaries, stenographers & typists	3,574,000	4,383,000	4,678,000	22.6	30.9
Secretaries	2,319,000	2,807,000	3,007,000	21.0	29.6
Stenographers	262,000	322,000	341,000	22.8	30.2
Typists	993,000	1,255,000	1,330,000	26.4	34.0
Shipping & receiving clerks	378,000	448,000	488,000	28.9	19.4
Shipping packers	340,000	398,000	431,000	17.1	26.9
Statement clerks	30,000	44,000	45,000	45.8	49.6
Statistical clerks	81,000	95,000	101,000	16.8	24.1
Stock clerks, stockroom & warehouse	787,000	964,000	1,043,000	22.4	32.5
Survey workers	40,000	48,000	52,000	17.8	27.7
Switchboard operators/ receptionists	219,000	276,000	298,000	26.0	36.1
Teacher's aides, except monitors	404,000	497,000	500,000	23.0	23.8
Telephone operators	312,000	376,000	414,000	20.6	32.6
Switchboard operators	171,000	218,000	234,000	27.6	37.2
Central office operators	101,000	113,000	128,000	11.2	26.1
Directory assistance operators	35,000	40,000	45,000	13.5	28.6
Ticket agents	49,000	51,000	54,000	3.7	10.1
Town clerks	26,000	33,000	34,000	28.5	30.8
Weighers	35,000	42,000	45,000	17.9	26.9
Crafts & related workers	11,679,000	14,366,000	15,555,000	23.0	33.2
Construction craft workers	2,950,000	3,747,000	4,037,000	27.0	36.8
Brick masons	144,000	204,000	220,000	41.7	52.8
Carpenters	979,000	1,183,000	1,274,000	20.8	30.2
Carpet cutters & layers	50,000	65,000	72,000	29.4	43.3
Ceiling tile installers & floor layers	25,000	35,000	38,000	36.9	50.7
Concrete and terrazzo finishers	113,000	152,000	164,000	34.6	45.0
Dry wall installers & lathers	92,000	125,000	135,000	35.5	46.2
Dry wall applicators	51,000	70,000	76,000	39.2	50.5
Tapers	30,000	42,000	46,000	40.7	51.7

Occupation	1978, Actual	Employment* 1990, Low Projection	1990, High Projection	% Change, 1978–90 Low	High
Electricians	516,000	678,000	726,000	31.4	40.8
Glaziers	35,000	48,000	51,000	35.5	44.6
Painters, construction & maintenance	363,000	436,000	477,000	20.0	31.3
Plumbers & pipefitters	375,000	492,000	526,000	31.1	40.0
Roofers	99,000	130,000	139,000	31.0	40.1
Structural steel workers	67,000	90,000	95,000	33.1	40.6
Mechanics, repairers & installers	3,758,000	4,764,000	5,157,000	26.8	37.2
Air conditioning, heating & refrigeration mechanics	165,000	213,000	230,000	29.0	39.1
Aircraft mechanics	97,000	125,000	133,000	28.3	36.2
Auto body repairers	154,000	189,000	201,000	22.7	30.4
Automotive mechanics	847,000	1,052,000	1,124,000	24.2	32.7
Coin machine servicers & repairers	27,000	29,000	31,000	9.5	16.4
Data processing machine mechanics	63,000	156,000	172,000	147.6	173.0
Diesel mechanics	166,000	214,000	227,000	29.3	37.2
Electric power line installers & repairers	157,000	189,000	215,000	20.3	36.5
Cable splicers	40,000	48,000	54,000	18.5	34.1
Line installers & repairers	110,000	133,000	151,000	21.3	37.4
Engineering equipment mechanics	86,000	104,000	112,000	20.8	30.4
Gas & electric appliance repairers	57,000	70,000	78,000	21.4	35.3
Instrument repairers	36,000	42,000	45,000	14.6	24.0
Maintenance mechanics	346,000	411,000	439,000	18.8	27.1
Maintenance repairers, general utility	626,000	785,000	846,000	25.5	35.2
Millwrights	93,000	108,000	114,000	15.5	22.4
Office machine & cash register servicers	49,900	89,000	96,000	80.8	96.2

Radio & television repairers	81,000	112,000	122,000	37.6	49.6
Railroad car repairers	30,000	24,000	27,000	−18.8	−10.5
Telephone installers & repairers	228,000	273,000	310,000	20.2	36.3
Central office repairers	47,000	56,000	63,000	19.4	35.3
Installers, repairers & section maintainers	69,000	83,000	94,000	20.4	36.3
Station installers	55,000	65,000	74,000	19.6	35.6
Metalworking craft workers, except mechanics	909,000	1,081,000	1,192,000	19.0	31.1
Boilermakers	42,000	52,000	57,000	25.6	36.7
Heat treaters, annealers & temperers	25,000	29,000	32,000	16.1	25.8
Machine tool setters, metalworking	57,000	66,000	74,000	16.1	29.8
Machinists	272,000	323,000	358,000	18.8	31.7
Sheet metal workers & tinsmiths	205,000	261,000	280,000	27.6	36.9
Tool & die makers	166,000	192,000	221,000	16.0	33.1
Printing trades craft workers	386,000	442,000	476,000	14.7	43.5
Compositors & typesetters	123,000	121,000	130,000	−1.9	6.0
Press & plate printers	168,000	197,000	211,000	17.4	25.9
Letter press operators	36,000	39,000	42,000	9.0	17.9
Offset lithographic press operators	75,000	92,000	99,000	22.5	31.9
Press operators & plate printers	35,000	41,000	43,000	16.1	21.8
Other crafts & related workers	3,677,000	4,332,000	4,693,000	17.8	27.6
Bakers	60,000	72,000	76,000	20.1	27.2
Blue-collar worker supervisors	1,274,000	1,495,000	1,616,000	17.4	26.9
Cabinetmakers	72,000	89,000	95,000	23.0	31.0
Crane, derrick & hoist operators	126,000	146,000	157,000	15.7	23.7

Occupation	1978, Actual	Employment* 1990, Low Projection	1990, High Projection	% Change, 1978–90 Low	High
Dental lab technicians	48,000	69,000	79,000	44.9	67.0
Furniture upholsterers	30,000	38,000	43,000	27.3	41.8
Heavy equipment operators	431,000	546,000	598,000	26.6	38.6
Inspectors	475,000	544,000	595,000	14.7	25.4
Jewelers & silversmiths	29,000	32,000	35,000	10.7	21.5
Merchandise displayers & window trimmers	26,000	31,000	33,000	17.8	26.3
Opticians	30,000	42,000	46,000	38.6	50.6
Sewage plant operators	38,000	43,000	45,000	15.0	18.3
Stationary engineers	60,000	68,000	72,000	13.5	19.9
Tailors	66,000	75,000	83,000	14.3	25.0
Testers	105,000	120,000	130,000	14.5	23.8
Water treatment plant operators	27,000	32,000	33,000	16.0	21.1
Operatives	14,205,000	16,399,000	17,697,000	15.4	24.6
Assemblers	1,672,000	1,997,000	2,192,000	19.4	31.1
Electrical & electronic assemblers	207,000	278,000	305,000	34.2	47.3
Electro-mechanical equipment assemblers	53,000	69,000	78,000	29.9	46.4
Machine assemblers	100,000	124,000	144,000	24.8	44.7
Bindery operatives	81,000	86,000	94,000	6.6	15.6
Bindery workers, assembly	41,000	43,000	47,000	6.6	16.0
Laundering, drycleaning & pressing machine operators	316,000	356,000	404,000	12.5	27.8
Laundry operators, small establishment	34,000	48,000	53,000	39.6	56.0
Pressers:					
Hand	30,000	32,000	36,000	7.2	19.3
Machine	54,000	56,000	65,000	2.4	18.8
Machine, laundry	66,000	74,000	84,000	11.8	26.6
Washers, machine & starchers	56,000	79,000	87,000	41.4	55.7

Metalworking operatives	1,650,000	1,970,000	2,211,000	19.4	34.0
Drill press & boring machine operators	123,000	148,000	167,000	19.6	35.4
Electroplaters	35,000	44,000	48,000	24.4	34.6
Grinding & abrading machine operators, metal	131,000	154,000	173,000	17.4	32.4
Lathe machine operators, metal	153,000	186,000	210,000	20.0	37.7
Machine tool operators:					
Combination	170,000	200,000	226,000	33.4	21.5
Numerical control	49,000	61,000	70,000	24.2	41.5
Tool room	40,000	46,000	52,000	15.3	31.6
Milling & planing machine operators	68,000	83,000	95,000	21.6	39.6
Power brake & bending machine operators, metal	41,000	48,000	54,000	19.0	32.3
Punch press operators, metal	195,000	217,000	240,000	11.2	23.0
Welders & flamecutters	570,000	696,000	784,000	22.1	37.6
Mine operatives not elsewhere classified	170,000	239,000	259,000	41.0	52.7
Roustabouts	61,000	81,000	85,000	31.4	37.9
Packing & inspecting operatives	906,000	981,000	1,041,000	8.3	14.9
Baggers	215,000	238,000	250,000	10.6	16.3
Production packagers	612,000	661,000	704,000	7.9	15.1
Selectors, glasswares	32,000	35,000	35,000	8.8	10.9
Painters, manufactured articles	166,000	205,000	222,000	23.4	33.5
Painters, automotive	40,000	56,000	59,000	40.0	46.0
Painters, production	113,000	132,000	145,000	17.3	29.0
Sewers & stitchers	919,000	967,000	1,065,000	5.2	15.9
Sewing machine operators:					
Regular equipment, garment	616,000	634,000	702,000	3.0	14.0
Special equipment, garment	89,000	96,000	106,000	8.6	20.0

Occupation	1978, Actual	Employment* 1990, Low Projection	1990, High Projection	% Change, 1978–90 Low	High
Regular equipment, nongarment	144,000	161,000	175,000	12.1	21.2
Special equipment, nongarment	40,000	45,000	49,000	13.1	21.7
Textile operatives	394,000	399,000	419,000	1.4	6.5
Folders, hand	27,000	29,000	32,000	8.6	19.3
Spinners, frame	31,000	32,000	32,000	1.4	4.2
Weavers	37,000	33,000	33,000	−11.2	−8.8
Transport equipment operatives	3,468,000	4,152,000	4,428,000	19.7	27.7
Ambulance drivers & attendants	28,000	41,000	42,000	45.3	48.8
Bus drivers	266,000	326,000	329,000	22.5	23.8
Chauffeurs	39,000	48,000	52,000	24.6	34.1
Delivery & route workers	802,000	916,000	991,000	14.3	23.5
Industrial truck operators	408,000	459,000	493,000	12.5	20.7
Parking attendants	37,000	44,000	51,000	21.6	40.2
Railroad brake operators	74,000	67,000	73,000	−10.3	−1.3
Taxi drivers	79,000	69,000	78,000	−12.6	−0.9
Truck drivers	1,672,000	2,110,000	2,246,000	26.2	34.3
All other operatives	4,311,000	4,882,000	5,189,000	13.2	20.4
Asbestos & insulation workers	42,000	58,000	62,000	37.7	47.3
Cutters, machine	29,000	32,000	34,000	9.9	16.9
Dressmakers, except factory	53,000	49,000	53,000	−8.3	−0.5
Filers, grinders, buffers & chippers	127,000	151,000	168,000	19.6	33.0
Fuel pump attendants & lubricators	434,000	475,000	492,000	9.5	13.4
Furnace operators & tenders, except metal	62,000	65,000	67,000	5.0	9.1
Stationary boiler firers	47,000	51,000	53,000	6.8	11.0

Miscellaneous machine operatives:				
Lumber & furniture	51,000	59,000	60,000	16.2	18.4
Chemicals & allied products	153,000	167,000	176,000	9.1	15.2
Rubber & miscellaneous plastics	229,000	284,000	292,000	24.0	27.7
Miscellaneous operatives not elsewhere classified:				
Durable goods	103,000	123,000	128,000	19.3	24.6
Nondurable goods	249,000	257,000	275,000	3.1	10.5
Mixing operatives	53,000	51,000	55,000	−2.4	4.3
Oilers	40,000	48,000	52,000	19.5	30.0
Photographic process workers	66,000	81,000	89,000	22.7	34.6
Rotary drill operator helpers	31,000	42,000	45,000	34.0	41.3
Shear & slitter operators, metal	32,000	37,000	40,000	15.5	26.4
Shoemaking machine operators	68,000	54,000	59,000	−20.0	−13.1
Surveyor helpers	48,000	68,000	70,000	39.9	45.2
Tire changers & repairers	60,000	71,000	77,000	17.5	27.2
Winding operatives not elsewhere classified	48,000	58,000	62,000	21.9	30.4
Coil winders	29,000	37,000	40,000	27.3	39.5
Wirers, electronic	28,000	35,000	38,000	24.5	36.1
Wood machinists	27,000	33,000	34,000	23.7	27.8
Service Workers	14,414,000	18,946,000	20,074,000	31.4	39.3
Food service workers	5,610,000	7,774,000	8,192,000	38.6	46.0
Bakers, bread & pastry	45,000	57,000	59,000	27.1	33.2
Bartenders	347,000	453,000	480,000	30.3	38.0
Butchers & meat cutters	178,000	212,000	225,000	18.6	25.8
Cooks, except private household	1,024,000	1,367,000	1,438,000	35.5	40.5
Cooks, institutional	296,000	370,000	386,000	25.2	30.7
Cooks, restaurant	320,000	445,000	471,000	39.2	47.4
Cooks, short order & specialty fast foods	408,000	552,000	580,000	35.1	42.1

Occupation	1978, Actual	Employment* 1990, Low Projection	1990, High Projection	% Change, 1978–90 Low	High
Food preparation & service workers, fast-food restaurant	714,000	1,206,000	1,265,000	68.8	77.1
Hosts/hostesses, restaurant, lounge, coffee shop	104,000	154,000	163,000	48.6	57.1
Kitchen helpers	771,000	1,072,000	1,131,000	39.0	46.7
Pantry, sandwich & coffee makers	64,000	92,000	97,000	43.1	51.8
Waiters/waitresses	1,539,000	2,071,000	2,186,000	34.6	42.1
Waiters' assistants	252,000	363,000	384,000	43.7	52.2
Janitors & sextons	2,585,000	3,257,000	3,504,000	26.0	35.5
Selected health service workers	1,251,000	1,921,000	2,051,000	53.5	63.9
Medical assistants	81,000	116,000	123,000	44.2	52.3
Nurses' aides & orderlies	1,089,000	1,683,000	1,801,000	54.6	65.4
Psychiatric aides	77,000	115,000	120,000	49.5	56.2
Selected personal service workers	1,547,000	2,028,000	2,206,000	31.1	42.6
Barbers	114,000	142,000	160,000	24.0	40.1
Child-care attendants	35,000	55,000	60,000	56.3	67.8
Child-care workers	398,000	581,000	615,000	46.1	54.5
Cosmetologists & women's hair stylists	434,000	530,000	603,000	22.2	38.9
Elevator operators	45,000	59,000	64,000	30.7	40.9
Flight attendants	51,000	64,000	68,000	26.8	34.6
Game & ride operators & concession workers	28,000	37,000	38,000	33.1	35.8
Housekeepers, hotel & motel	49,000	67,000	74,000	35.7	50.9
Recreation facility attendants	65,000	83,000	85,000	28.3	31.0
Reducing instructors	26,000	29,000	35,000	12.2	35.8
School monitors	37,000	38,000	38,000	3.0	3.4

Ushers, lobby attendants & ticket takers	40,000	46,000	46,000	15.4	14.5
Welfare service aides	84,000	126,000	132,000	51.1	57.2
Protective service workers	1,586,000	2,098,000	2,189,000	32.3	38.0
Correction officials & jailers	95,000	152,000	154,000	60.3	63.1
Crossing or bridge tenders	27,000	32,000	33,000	18.1	20.8
Crossing guards, school	38,000	48,000	49,000	28.5	30.8
Firefighters	200,000	256,000	260,000	27.6	29.9
Fire officers	46,000	59,000	60,000	28.6	30.8
Guards & doorkeepers	591,000	801,000	868,000	35.5	46.8
Police detectives	59,000	72,000	74,000	23.1	25.3
Police officers	94,000	119,000	121,000	26.7	28.9
Police patrolmen/women	358,000	459,000	467,000	28.0	30.3
Private household workers	1,160,000	982,000	993,000	−15.4	−14.4
Child care workers, private household	486,000	412,000	417,000	−15.3	−14.3
Housekeepers, private household	118,000	100,000	101,000	−15.4	−14.4
Maids & servants, private household	530,000	449,000	455,000	−15.2	−14.2
Supervisors, nonworking, service	189,000	254,000	270,000	34.1	42.3
All other service workers	484,000	633,000	670,000	30.8	38.3
Laborers, except farm	5,902,000	6,955,000	7,441,000	17.8	26.1
Animal caretakers	88,000	113,000	122,000	27.6	38.2
Construction laborers, excluding carpenter helpers	277,000	348,000	365,000	25.7	31.7
Highway maintenance workers	170,000	211,000	215,000	24.4	26.6
Pipelayers	43,000	54,000	60,000	25.5	38.3
Reinforcing-iron workers	31,000	42,000	45,000	34.5	41.5

Occupation	1978, Actual	Employment* 1990, Low Projection	1990, High Projection	% Change, 1978–90 Low	High
Cannery workers	82,000	80,000	84,000	−2.5	3.2
Cleaners, vehicle	118,000	150,000	159,000	27.0	35.1
Conveyor operators & tenders	55,000	62,000	68,000	13.8	24.0
Garbage collectors	110,000	137,000	148,000	24.4	34.4
Gardeners & groundskeepers, except farm	639,000	738,000	789,000	15.6	23.5
Helpers, trades	928,000	1,161,000	1,255,000	25.0	35.2
Line service attendants	27,000	32,000	34,000	17.7	25.5
Off-bearers	25,000	28,000	28,000	9.7	10.8
Riggers	28,000	33,000	35,000	17.0	24.7
Stock handlers	918,000	1,131,000	1,210,000	23.2	31.8
Order fillers	352,000	407,000	445,000	15.5	26.2
Stock clerks, sales floor	566,000	724,000	766,000	27.9	35.3
Timbercutting & logging workers	70,000	59,000	63,000	−16.0	−10.9
Fallers & buckers	43,000	36,000	38,000	−16.6	−11.5
Farmers & farmworkers	2,775,000	2,193,000	2,426,000	−21.0	−12.6
Farmers & farm managers	1,486,000	1,231,000	1,355,000	−17.2	−8.8
Farmers (owners & tenants)	1,445,000	1,200,000	1,321,000	−17.0	−8.6
Farm managers	41,000	31,000	34,000	−25.0	−15.8
Farm supervisors & laborers	1,289,000	963,000	1,071,000	−25.3	−16.9
Farm supervisors	32,000	25,000	28,000	−22.4	−13.0
Farm laborers	1,257,000	938,000	1,044,000	−25.4	−17.0